Cambridge Elements ☰

Elements in Religion and Violence
edited by
James R. Lewis
University of Tromsø
Margo Kitts
Hawai'i Pacific University

THE BAHÁ'Í FAITH, VIOLENCE, AND NON-VIOLENCE

Robert H. Stockman
Wilmette Institute

T0349612

CAMBRIDGE
UNIVERSITY PRESS

CAMBRIDGE
UNIVERSITY PRESS

University Printing House, Cambridge CB2 8BS, United Kingdom

One Liberty Plaza, 20th Floor, New York, NY 10006, USA

477 Williamstown Road, Port Melbourne, VIC 3207, Australia

314–321, 3rd Floor, Plot 3, Splendor Forum, Jasola District Centre,
New Delhi – 110025, India

79 Anson Road, #06–04/06, Singapore 079906

Cambridge University Press is part of the University of Cambridge.

It furthers the University's mission by disseminating knowledge in the pursuit of
education, learning, and research at the highest international levels of excellence.

www.cambridge.org
Information on this title: www.cambridge.org/9781108706278
DOI: 10.1017/9781108613446

First published 2020

A catalogue record for this publication is available from the British Library.

ISBN 978-1-108-70627-8 Paperback
ISSN 2397-9496 (online)
ISSN 2514-3786 (print)

The Bahá'í Faith, Violence, and Non-violence

Elements in Religion and Violence

DOI: 10.1017/9781108613446

First published online: July 2020

Robert H. Stockman

Wilmette Institute

Author for correspondence: Robert H. Stockman, rstockman@usbnc.org

ABSTRACT: Both violence and non-violence are important themes in the Bahá'í Faith, but their relationship is not simple. The Bahá'í sacred writings see violence in the world – not just against Bahá'ís, but physical and structural violence against everyone – as being a consequence of the immature state of human civilization. The Bahá'í community itself has been non-violent since its founding by Bahá'u'lláh in the mid-nineteenth century and has developed various strategies for responding to persecution non-violently. This Element explores how the Bahá'í scriptures provide a blueprint for building a new, more mature, culture and civilization on this planet where violence will be rare and non-violence prevalent.

KEYWORDS: Bahá'í Faith, violence, non-violence, jihad, unity

ISBNs: 9781108706278 (PB), 9781108613446 (OC)

ISSNs: 2397-9496 (online), 2514-3786 (print)

Contents

1 The Forerunner Movement: The Bábí Faith   2

2 The Writings of the Báb   4

3 The Bábí Community and Persecution   6

4 Mírzá Ḥusayn-ʿAlí of Núr, Bahá'u'lláh   8

5 Other References about Violence and Non-violence   21

6 Bahá'u'lláh and ʿAbdu'l-Bahá about Oneness and Unity   24

7 Building Unity through Organization   31

8 The Authority of Bahá'í Institutions: The Covenant   36

9 Consultation   37

10 Disciplining Members   39

11 Persecution of the Bahá'í Community   40

12 Bahá'í Teachings for Preventing Violence
    at a Societal and Global Level   44

13 Growth and Development of the International
    Bahá'í Community, 1892–Present   50

14 Constructive Resilience in Iran   61

15 Constructive Engagement   63

16 Conclusion   64

    Bibliography   66

Both violence and non-violence are important themes in the Bahá'í Faith, but their relationship is not straightforward. Violence – in the form of persecution of the Bahá'í community – is an ongoing theme in Bahá'í history, one that continues today in Iran, Yemen, and a smattering of other nations. Non-violence is a central corollary to the major principles of Bahá'í theology, which seeks to create a world of justice where violence is absolutely minimized, discriminatory treatment is eliminated, justice reigns, and opportunity for all is abundant.

But it would not be correct to attribute the Bahá'í emphasis on non-violence to be a consequence of its experience of violence. Rather, the Bahá'í scriptures[1] see violence in the world – not just against Bahá'ís, but against everyone – as being a consequence of the immature state of human society and culture. The Bahá'í scriptures claim to offer principles for transforming human character and for building a new, more mature culture and civilization where violence is minimized or eliminated. In particular, the

---

[1] The Bahá'í scriptures constitute the writings of the 'Alí-Muhammad of Shiraz, titled Báb (1819–50), Mírzá Husayn-'Alí of Núr, titled Bahá'u'lláh (1817–92), and 'Abbás Effendi, titled 'Abdu'l-Bahá (1844–1921). The first two men claimed to be Manifestations of God, messengers infallibly empowered to deliver divine revelation to humanity. The third was Bahá'u'lláh's son, who said 'Abdu'l-Bahá was the Faith's authoritative and infallible interpreter. The literary corpus of each is vast: 2,000, 18,000, and 30,000 extant works respectively, involving at least 5 million, 6 million, and 5 million words respectively. While the Báb wrote numerous treatises and books, all three wrote books, essays, poetry, and especially letters, which form the bulk of their writing. They wrote in Persian, Arabic, and in a complex literary mix of both. Bahá'u'lláh and 'Abdu'l-Bahá also wrote tablets to Zoroastrians in "pure Persian" – that is, Persian with no use of Arabic words. 'Abdu'l-Bahá wrote in Ottoman Turkish as well. In addition to the Bahá'í scriptures, Shoghi Effendi Rabbani (1897–1957), as Guardian of the Bahá'í Faith, wrote 36,000 works, almost all letters, totaling over 5 million words, and the Universal House of Justice, the current head of the Faith, has written or overseen the writing of innumerable letters, statements, cables, and emails. The writings of Shoghi Effendi and the Universal House of Justice are not considered scripture, but they are authoritative texts (as are the scriptural works). Its vast literary corpus is an important aspect of the Bahá'í Faith to understand.

scriptures seek to define the values of a world where structural violence – social structures that perpetuate inequity and injustice, thereby causing preventable suffering – have been eliminated.[2] They go on to state that "God's purpose for sending His Prophets" has always been "twofold": to free humanity from the "darkness of ignorance"; and to "ensure the peace and tranquility of mankind, and to provide all the means by which they can be established." They urge human beings to "regard ye not one another as strangers. Ye are the fruits of one tree, and the leaves of one branch." They even say that "religion must be conducive to love and unity among mankind; for if it be the cause of enmity and strife, the absence of religion is preferable."[3]

1 The Forerunner Movement: The Bábí Faith

The Bahá'í Faith and its antecedent movement, the Bábí Faith, arose from the Shí'í Islam of nineteenth-century Iran[4] and was fiercely opposed by the clergy and eventually the government of the country, resulting in the deaths of thousands of believers. The founder, 'Alí-Muhammad of Shiraz (1819–50), who took the title of the Báb, made the claim that he was the Qá'im or Return of the Twelfth Imám, the messianic figure expected by the Twelver Shí'ís then dominating Iran. He began his movement on May 22, 1844, at

---

[2] There are various definitions of structural violence. Here I refer to the work of Johan Gultang. See "What Is Social Violence" for a simple overview at www.thoughtco.com/structural-violence-4174956.

[3] Bahá'u'lláh, *Gleanings from the Writings of Bahá'u'lláh*, 79–80; Bahá'u'lláh, *Tablets of Bahá'u'lláh Revealed After the Kitáb-i-Aqdas*, 164; 'Abdu'l-Baha, *The Promulgation of Universal Peace*, 127.

[4] Upon the death of Muhammad (632 CE) Islam split into two major divisions, one maintaining that Muhammad had appointed his cousin and son-in-law 'Alí to be his successor as Imám ("leader") of the Faith, the other maintaining that the community could choose a Caliph ("successor" or "deputy") to lead them. Throughout most of Islamic history, the Shi'ites have been the minority. Since the sixteenth century they have dominated Iran. The form of Shi'ism in that country maintains that Muhammad was succeeded by twelve infallible and sinless Imáms, and that the twelfth one will return at the end of time.

the age of twenty-four. In the next six years he gradually and progressively revealed his claim in his extensive writings – thousands of letters, Qur'án commentaries, treatises, and prayers, of which over 2,000 works and 5 million words are still extant – to be a Manifestation of God of stature as great as Muhammad, receiving revelation as profound as the Qur'án.[5]

Such a polarizing message both attracted and repelled. Some seminarians were enchanted by the power of the Báb's writing in both Arabic and Persian and went out to proclaim the new faith, attracting perhaps a hundred thousand out of Iran's population of around 5 million. Urban merchants, artisans, and the poor became his followers. Some villagers converted, usually through members of their local mosque. Rural tribesmen were less successfully reached. Notably, at least one Iranian Jew and one Iranian Zoroastrian converted, which reflected the faith's desire to reach beyond religious difference and create a diverse community. The teachings of the Báb were not known in detail, however, because only hand copies of a few of his writings were available – the Báb was imprisoned in 1845 – and there was no opportunity to organize communities because persecution began immediately.

The Shí'í clergy were the immediate opponents of the Bábí movement because the Báb's messianic claim, if accepted, would have stripped them of their authority. Islam had a long history of false claimants who often used their claim to foment rebellion. Under pressure from the clergy, the royal government put the Báb under house arrest in 1845, transferred him to remote castles in the mountains of Azerbaijan in the northwestern corner of the country in 1847, put him on trial for blasphemy in 1848, and executed him in 1850. The Bábí community was under able leadership at first from several of the "Letters of the Living" the Báb had appointed, and they circulated hand copies of what writings of his they had. They were also able to maintain limited correspondence with him and on one occasion one was even able to visit him.

---

[5] The Bahá'í authoritative texts use the terms prophet, messenger, and Manifestation somewhat interchangeably, but nevertheless recognize a distinction between the major prophets who establish a new religion (like Moses) and lesser prophets who work under the shadow of a major prophet (like Isaiah or Ezekiel). In this essay, the term "Manifestation" is restricted in use to refer to the founders of religions only.

2 The Writings of the Báb

The Báb's writings as they relate to violence and non-violence have been subject to various interpretations. They contain the Arabic word *jihád*, which literally means "struggle or striving to achieve something." In Islam it carries a multitude of meanings including striving to serve God and control one's ego and passions; non-violent defense of one's faith through such efforts as preaching and writing; defensive military action to protect the Muslim community from violent attack; and, finally, offensive warfare against an enemy of the Faith. In Islam it is often divided into two types: an inner moral or spiritual struggle; and an outer struggle, usually using arms.

In his earlier writings the Báb often endorsed basic Islamic teachings (including jihád) so that "the people might not be seized with perturbation."[6] But his later writings (1848–50), in particular the Persian Bayán, the principal repository of the Báb's legal teachings – the main source of the Bábí sharí'ah – provides a complex elaboration on the subject of jihád. Initially, the writings appeared to endorse violence, but they subjected it to so many restrictions as to render it impossible and countered it with numerous peaceable, moral strivings. Among the commandments in the Bayán, for example, the Báb commands that all non-Bábís be expelled from the five main provinces of Iran, that their property be confiscated, and that their books be burned. But the Báb adds that no individual Bábí can initiate such a jihád. Instead it is conditioned on two prerequisites: "the exaltation of the Cause of the Báb"; and that a Bábí state had already been created. The Báb also says that the "exaltation" of his cause will follow after the "exaltation" of the cause of the Promised One, who would appear in nine or nineteen years after him. In other words, the Báb anticipated that another Manifestation would appear first and that such a Manifestation would succeed to spread his cause. Such a Manifestation would also have the divine authority to accept or nullify all the Báb's teachings. Consequently, the Báb appears to have created purely symbolic principles of violent jihád – ones that could never be utilized by the Bábís themselves – as a way to use existing Islamic principles to point to the coming of his successor.[7] In many of the Báb's

---

[6] The Báb, Dalá'il-i-Sab'ih, in *Selections from the Writings of the Báb*, 119.

[7] Nader Saiedi, *Gate of the Heart*, 364.

later works he wrote extensively about the importance of the next Manifestation of God, whom he referred to as "He whom God shall make manifest." He implied the Manifestation would be called "Bahá" and enjoined acceptance of him in no uncertain terms.

The teachings related to violent jihád are actually a small portion of the Bayán. The bulk of the work elaborates on the basic ethical principle that, even if people wrong you, you must forgive them, do good to them, and behave toward them as God would when he gives grace to those who ungratefully repudiate Him. In short, they call for an inner jihád of spiritual transformation.[8] One must be content with God, with the laws of God, with one's parents, and with oneself. The Báb calls for perfection and refinement in a variety of senses: in keeping rivers pure and unpolluted; in producing crafts and goods of the highest quality; in building beautiful dwellings with doors high enough for even the tallest person to enter; in the creation of beautiful art; in bathing regularly; in wearing clean and spotless clothing; in the spread of prosperity to all; and even in the drinking of tea. He forbade causing grief and sadness to anyone and said this was "doubly binding" in the treatment of women, implying a new status of women in society. He also forbade the physical punishment and humiliation of children. The Báb saw all of these actions as expressions of the beauty and virtue of God in one's life and as forms of worship.[9] He sought to spiritualize one's understanding of the world, including a symbolic description of time itself through the introduction of a calendar of nineteen months, each with nineteen days, with the days and months named after attributes of God.[10] In short, the Báb sought to create an entirely new sort of community, one focused on unity, love, and service to others and one where there would be no role for violence, except perhaps occasionally in the restraint of criminals. In this

---

[8] Saiedi, *Gate of the Heart*, 302–3.   [9] Saiedi, *Gate of the Heart*, 303–25.

[10] The Badí' calendar established by the Báb and accepted by Bahá'u'lláh is the standard calendar used by the Bahá'í Faith today. It has nineteen months of nineteen days (which total 361 days) with four additional days to bring the total to 365 days (five additional days in a leap year). Months are named for attributes of God such as Bahá (splendor), Jalál (glory), Jamál (beauty), 'Azamat (grandeur), Núr (light), etc.

larger context of love and peace, any teachings about violent jihád are utterly incongruous.

While the Báb did not outright proclaim a new status for women, he did recognize one woman as a member of his inner circle of disciples, one of the nineteen Letters of the Living. Ṭáhirih (ca. 1814–52) came to play a very prominent role in the leadership. She was one of the three hosts at an important conference of prominent Bábís at a hamlet named Badasht, which had as one of its purposes the implementation of the teachings in the Bayán. She understood that implementation of the Bayán meant a break with Islam. One day she appeared unveiled before the men of the gathering, proclaiming that it was a new day. One man, shocked by her exposed face, slit his own throat and ran from the meeting. Others immediately abandoned the Bábí Faith and left. But for most it was the decisive event that proclaimed their independence from the Islamic sharíʿah. The fact that a woman brought about the break from Islam has become an important fact for Bahá'ís, as is the fact that the conference occurred just weeks before the Seneca Falls Convention in upstate New York, which symbolically marked the beginning of the struggle for women's rights in the United States. Ṭáhirih's last words, right before she was strangled to death for being a prominent Bábí in 1852, allegedly were "You can kill me as soon as you like, but you cannot stop the emancipation of women."[11] The significance of the emancipation of woman to the issue of violence is twofold: first, that women are often the greatest recipients of physical violence, and their emancipation is a factor in the reduction of that violence; second, that it is impossible to create a society free of structural violence as long as women are oppressed.

3 The Bábí Community and Persecution

The Bábí community's familiarity with the Báb's teachings was limited by its very short duration (six years from the Báb's declaration to his execution), its lack of access to his writings, and the severe persecution

---

[11] Shoghi Effendi, *God Passes By*, 32–3, 75; Nabíl-i-Zarandí, *The Dawn-Breakers*, 293–6.

it soon faced. In two small cities – Zanján in northern Iran and Nayríz in the south – mosque leaders became Bábís, they were followed into the Bábí Faith by their congregations, and as a result, an entire urban quarter became Bábí. In the case of Zanján, the Bábís were Turkic speaking and followers of Akhbári Shí'ism, rather than the Usúlí Shí'ísm that dominated the rest of Iran, so preexisting ethnic and religious differences were involved. In both cities, opposition forced the Bábís to barricade themselves into their quarter and defend themselves, the army arrived, a bloody siege of many months ensued, and thousands of men, women, and children lost their lives.

A third upheaval wiped out much of the movement's remaining leadership. In early 1848, Mullá Husayn, the most important of the Letters of the Living, met with the Báb in his castle imprisonment in northwestern Iran and then went to the city of Mashhad in the far northeastern corner of Iran to proclaim the *qiyáma* or "Day of Resurrection." Notably, no violent jihád was declared by the Báb or his followers. Quddús, the other leading Letter of the Living, set out westward from Mashhad in June 1848 with a band of men flying the black standard, a flag denoting the latter days. As they marched westward they were joined by other Bábís and by excited converts. In October, as they reached the forests along the Caspian Sea, Iran's shah died in Tehran, and the new shah was frightened that their symbolic act demonstrating the start of the latter days would initiate a rebellion. Eventually the band of men, led by Mullá Husayn and Quddús, was forced to stop, defend itself, and fortify itself in an ancient shrine to a prominent scholar named Shaykh Tabarsí. An army of 12,000 men pinned them down. Their sorties into the army camp allowed them to capture ammunition and supplies and demoralize the professional army. After a six-month siege that claimed the lives of both Mullá Husayn and Quddús, the survivors surrendered on the promise that they would be allowed to go free, but the army massacred them instead.

All three cases – Nayríz, Zanján, and Shaykh Tabarsí – involved defensive action on the part of Bábis, who were surrounded and under attack from the Iranian army. They were essentially examples of defensive jihád as would be practiced in Islam, though no jihád was declared. The symbolic power of their sacrifice for the new religion was not lost on subsequent generations, however, and their stories have been transmuted into glorious examples of martyrdom for the faith. They serve to inspire Bahá'ís right up to this day, not to go out and fight but rather to be living sacrifices in their service to Bahá'u'lláh.[12]

4 Mírzá Ḥusayn-ʿAlí of Núr, Bahá'u'lláh

One of the earliest followers of the Báb was Mírzá Ḥusayn-ʿAlí (1817–92), who later took the title of Bahá'u'lláh and founded the Bahá'í Faith. He was a member of the aristocratic class, his father being a minister of the Shah. Bahá'u'lláh turned down offers for various government positions and devoted himself to the care of Tehran's poor. In adulthood, Bahá'u'lláh wrote about a remarkable experience he had as a child. At one point he read a book about the Medina period of Muhammad's life and the betrayal of the defenses of that city by the Banú Qurayzah, a Jewish tribe, when the Meccans attacked. After the Meccans were unable to take Medina and returned home, the Banú Qurayzah were brought to justice for their treason. A judge who was otherwise a friend of the tribe decreed (possibly based on the commands to the Israelite army in Deuteronomy 20:12–14) that all the men should be beheaded and all their women, children, and property should be distributed to the Muslim army. Muhammad and the tribe accepted this decision, and Muhammad carried out the punishment. Bahá'u'lláh, however, was profoundly grieved and beseeched God "to bring about whatever would be the cause of love, fellowship, and unity among all the peoples of the earth." Before sunrise on his birthday (we are not told the year) he experienced a transformation that recurred repeatedly over the next twelve days, "after which waves of the sea of utterance became manifest and the effulgences of the orb of assurance shone forth until it culminated in the advent of His Revelation."[13]

---

[12] The story of the defenders of Nayríz, Zanján, and Shaykh Ṭabarsí was a central part of an early translation into English of *The Dawn-Breakers: Nabíl's Narrative of the Early Days of the Bahá'í Revelation*, a translation published specifically to inspire the Western Bahá'ís to serve their new religion.

[13] Bahá'u'lláh, quoted in Nader Saiedi, *Logos and Civilization*, 305.

In short, Bahá'u'lláh is saying that this event, apparently in his child-hood, triggered his first experience of revelation. This would have been years before the Báb declared his mission in 1844 and decades before the symbolic beginning of Bahá'u'lláh's mission in 1853 or his first public declaration of prophethood in 1863. The trigger was an event that repre-sented the divine will in the seventh century – the punishment of an entire tribe for treason in the midst of a violent, lawless world – but which was an ethically inadequate response based on the needs of the modern world.

Bahá'u'lláh goes on to note that his writings provided "that which is the cause of unity and fellowship."[14] By the time of his passing in 1892, he had composed at least 18,000 works (mostly letters, referred to as "tablets") totaling over 6 million words.[15] He is known to have composed tablets as early as 1848 at Badasht, but the oldest extant text, a mystic poem titled the Rashḥ-i-Amá (sometimes translated "Sprinklings from the Cloud of Unknowing"), dates to his imprisonment in the Black Pit of Tehran in late 1852. It marked the symbolic beginning of his ministry.

After his release from the Black Pit, Bahá'u'lláh was exiled to Ottoman Iraq, where he arrived in the spring of 1853. Because of contention caused by his half brother and disunity in the Bábí community of Baghdad, he left the city for two years in the mountains of Kurdistan, a period somewhat similar to Jesus's forty days in the wilderness. Upon his return to Baghdad in 1858, Bahá'u'lláh penned several significant works focusing on the spiritual journey of the believer. The Hidden Words provided a series of pithy ethical and spiritual aphorisms "revealed unto the Prophets of old" but "clothed" in the "garment of brevity." It called on people to "possess a pure kindly and radiant heart," noted that the "best beloved" of all things in God's sight is "justice," warned people to "breathe not the sins of others so long as thou art thyself a sinner," proclaimed death "a messenger of joy to thee," and reminded the believer to "busy not thyself with this world, for

---

[14] Bahá'u'lláh, quoted in Saiedi, *Logos and Civilization*, 305.

[15] The latest estimates of the quantity of writings created by the Báb, Bahá'u'lláh, and 'Abdu'l-Bahá, and currently available in the archives of the Bahá'í World Centre in Haifa, Israel, are found in the Research Department of the Universal House of Justice to the Universal House of Justice, October 1, 2010.

with fire We test the gold and with gold We test Our servants." It repeatedly emphasized that people are "noble" and "rich," that they are immortal, and that they can find the divine and all divine qualities within themselves. It rejected confession of one's sins to others and urged the believer to "bring thyself to account each day ere thou art summoned to a reckoning; for death, unheralded, shall come upon thee and thou shalt be called to give account for thy deeds."[16]

Bahá'u'lláh's mystic work called The Seven Valleys was revealed for Shaykh Muḥiyu'd-Dín, a Sufi of the Qádirí order. Structured similarly to Farídu'd-dín Aṭṭár's *The Conference of the Birds* and utilizing Sufi technical terminology, it described the seven "stages that mark the wayfarer's journey from the abode of dust to the heavenly homeland." The Four Valleys, a work revealed for yet another prominent Sufi, Shaykh 'Abdu'r-Raḥmán Tálabání of Kirkúk, noted that "those who progress in mystic wayfaring are of four kinds" and explored the nature of each.[17]

The Gems of Divine Mysteries continued on the theme of spiritual development, but it also explained how the Báb was the promised Qá'im of Shí'í Islam. It offered commentaries on qur'ánic and biblical texts and interpretations of such concepts as resurrection, the Day of Judgment, and life after death. The Kitáb-i-Íqán (The Book of Certitude), revealed in January 1861, capped this period of Bahá'u'lláh's life with a lengthy and extensive interpretation of qur'ánic and biblical prophecies, explanations about the crucial importance of prayer and fasting, and elucidation about the spiritual journey of the soul. A subtheme of the work is Bahá'u'lláh's messianic secret, hints of his future claim to be "He whom God shall make manifest," the messianic successor of the Báb.

An important subsection of the work, often called "The Tablet of the True Seeker," addresses the true nature of spiritual striving, jihád in the inner, personal, non-violent sense. In the original Persian one can see references to the one who conducts personal jihád, the *mujáhid*, as well as the qur'ánic term *jáhadú*, referring to "effort" or "striving":

[16] Bahá'u'lláh, Hidden Words, Arabic, nos. 1, 2, 27, 32, 55, 13, 14, 31.
[17] The Seven Valleys, 4; The Four Valleys, 49.

But, O my brother, when a true seeker [mujáhid, one who conducts jihád] determineth to take the step of search in the path leading to the knowledge of the Ancient of Days, he must, before all else, cleanse and purify his heart, which is the seat of the revelation of the inner mysteries of God, from the obscuring dust of all acquired knowledge, and the allusions of the embodiments of satanic fancy. He must purge his breast, which is the sanctuary of the abiding love of the Beloved, of every defilement, and sanctify his soul from all that pertaineth to water and clay, from all shadowy and ephemeral attachments. He must so cleanse his heart that no remnant of either love or hate may linger therein ... He must never seek to exalt himself above any one, must wash away from the tablet of his heart every trace of pride and vainglory, must cling unto patience and resignation, observe silence, and refrain from idle talk. ... That seeker should also regard backbiting as grievous error, and keep himself aloof from its dominion, inasmuch as backbiting quencheth the light of the heart, and extinguisheth the life of the soul. He should be content with little, and be freed from all inordinate desire. ... He should succour the dispossessed, and never withhold his favour from the destitute. He should show kindness to animals, how much more unto his fellow-man, to him who is endowed with the power of utterance. He should not hesitate to offer up his life for his Beloved, nor allow the censure of the people to turn him away from the Truth. ... He should forgive the sinful, and never despise his low estate, for none knoweth what his own end shall be. ... These are among the attributes of the exalted, and constitute the hall-mark of the spiritually-minded. They have already been mentioned in connection with the requirements of the wayfarers [sharáʿit-i mujáhidín wa mashy-i sálikín] that tread the Path of Positive Knowledge. When the detached wayfarer and sincere seeker hath fulfilled these essential conditions, then and only then can he be called a true seeker [mujáhid dar barih-yi 'ú ṣádiq mi'áyad]. Whensoever he hath fulfilled the conditions implied in the verse: "Whoso maketh efforts for Us" [alladhína jáhadú fína], he shall enjoy the blessing conferred by the words: "In Our ways shall We assuredly guide him." [Qur'án 29:69][18]

In these works, Bahá'u'lláh defined the heart of his future religion as the "mystical feeling that unites man with God." All religions have at their core a mystic striving, but as Moojan Momen has noted, in most religions only a minority of the followers focus on it in the form of monasticism, clericalism, or a lifelong mystic pursuit. For most, ritualistic or legalistic aspects of religion dominate. Bahá'u'lláh's goal appears to have been to minimize both ritualism and legalism and make mystic striving central in his religion in order to create strivers (mujáhid) focused on their ongoing spiritual transformation. Human beings are viewed not as captive to original sin, as in much of Christian theology, but as on an infinite path of progress in this world and the next, a personal path everyone must pray and meditate about and be responsible for. While human beings can never become perfect, this approach to striving focuses on their progress rather than dwelling on their sins and failures. It also asserts that, with the right understanding of spiritual and ethical principles, a religion of strivers can produce a civilization that is non-violent, in both the physical and structural senses.[19]

---

[18] Bahá'u'lláh, The Kitáb-i-Íqán, 192. I am indebted to Lawson, "The Return of Joseph and the Peaceable Imagination," 12–14, for the Persian and Arabic transliterations in this passage. The translation is an authoritative one by Shoghi Effendi and sometimes is not literal.

[19] Shoghi Effendi, quoted in Helen Hornby (comp.), *Lights of Guidance: A Bahá'í Reference File*, 2nd ed., New Delhi: Bahá'í Publishing Trust, 1988. Moojan Momen, "Mysticism and the Bahá'í Community," www.momen.org/bahai2/ mysticismbc.htm. The psychiatrist Hossain Danesh emphasizes the psychological importance of the Bahá'í concept of the nature of human beings, in contrast to the traditional Christian notion of the stain of sin on every human soul, in his monograph *The Violence-Free Society: A Gift for Our Children*.

On April 20, 1863, Bahá'u'lláh gathered with a small group of his closest followers in a garden called Riḍván in Baghdad, where he had settled after being exiled by the Iranian government. Over the next twelve days He announced his mission as a Manifestation of God, the one called "He whom God shall make manifest" by the Báb. In a tablet he wrote some years later, he summarized the three main principles he enunciated in the Riḍván garden. The first was that "in this Revelation the law of the sword hath been annulled." This referred not merely to that particular instrument of violence but to the prohibition of the use of violence in general. In the Islamic context it would refer to the use of violent jihád in the protection and propagation of the Faith. Instead, Bahá'u'lláh urged his followers to "unsheathe the sword of your tongue from the scabbard of utterance, for therewith ye can conquer the citadels of men's hearts." In the broader context of Bahá'u'lláh's other teachings, it refers to the construction of a society where the dignity and rights of all people are upheld.[20]

The second principle Bahá'u'lláh enunciated in the garden of Ridván was that there would be no future divine messenger, bearing a revelation from God, for at least a thousand years. This principle set a minimum duration for Bahá'u'lláh's mission and the implementation of his teachings. It implied the eventual coming of another Manifestation after the thousand-year period (in contrast to past religions, which often claim to be the final religion). It also implied the creation of a covenant with his followers.

The third principle was that at that moment "God, exalted be His Glory, shed the full splendour of all His Names upon all creation."[21] Bahá'u'lláh later explains that "all created things were immersed in the sea of purification when, on that first day of Riḍván, We shed upon the whole of creation the splendours of Our most excellent Names and Our most exalted Attributes."[22] Hence this principle appears to include the oneness of humanity: that no person or group was excluded from this new outpouring

---

[20] Bahá'u'lláh, *Days of Remembrance: Selections from the Writings of Bahá'u'lláh for the Bahá'í Holy Days*, 38; Saiedi, *Logos and Civilization*, 242, 245, 243.

[21] Bahá'u'lláh, *Days of Remembrance: Selections from the Writings of Bahá'u'lláh for the Bahá'í Holy Days*, 38; Saiedi, *Logos and Civilization*, 242.

[22] Bahá'u'lláh, Kitáb-i-Aqdas, para. 75.

of divine grace, and all were made pure and whole by it. This principle implied the desire to share the new religion with all the peoples of the Earth and build a diverse, inclusive community.

Bahá'u'lláh elaborated on these three principles in great detail over the next thirty years. From Baghdad, he was banished to Istanbul, the Ottoman capital, for four months, then to Edirne in late 1863. Starting in 1867, Bahá'u'lláh wrote a series of epistles to kings and prominent leaders, including Queen Victoria, Napoleon III, Kaiser Wilhelm, Tsar Alexander II, Sultan ʿAbduʾl-Azíz, Shah Násiruʾd-dín of Iran, and Pope Pius IX. To all of them, he proclaimed openly his claim to be the latest divine messenger. To the Pope, he specifically stated that he was the return of Christ ("He, verily, hath again come down from Heaven even as He came down from it the first time") and advised him to "sell all the embellished ornaments thou dost possess" and "abandon thy kingdom unto the kings" (Victor Emmanuel II having already conquered the papal states a few years earlier). Addressing Christian monks, he called them to come out of their churches and cloisters, instructed them to busy themselves "with what will profit you and others," forbade lechery to them, and commanded them to enter into wedlock.[23]

He warned Napoleon III that "for what thou hast done, thy kingdom shall be thrown into confusion, and thine empire shall pass from thine hands" just a year or so before the Franco-Prussian War overthrew him. He praised Queen Victoria for having abolished the slave trade and "entrusted the reins of counsel into the hands of the representatives of the people." In his hundreds of pages directed to the kings and rulers of the world, he called on them to reduce their armaments, stop excessive taxation of their citizens, cease to "rob them to rear palaces for yourselves," protect them from "the hands of the robber," pursue moderation, and ensure justice for their long-suffering people, who were their "treasures."[24] The purpose of the epistles was to give the world's leaders a formal opportunity to accept him, even if no acceptance was expected.

[23] Bahá'u'lláh, *The Summons of the Lord of Hosts*, 55, 62, 70.
[24] Bahá'u'lláh, *The Summons of the Lord of Hosts*, 72, 89, 90, 93.

Bahá'u'lláh also wrote extensively to the Bábís to state clearly his claim to be He whom God shall make manifest and to answer any objections they raised. As a result of this and other efforts, virtually the entire Bábí community became Bahá'ís over the next few years.

In the summer of 1868 Bahá'u'lláh was further exiled to Akka in Palestine (now northern Israel). He was confined there in a prison with his family and a group of close followers for two years and then released to live within the city walls. Eventually he was allowed to reside in a mansion outside town.

In 1873 Bahá'u'lláh penned the Kitáb-i-Aqdas or "Most Holy Book," his book of laws. Its lengthy preface noted that every person had the "twin duties" of recognizing the Manifestation of God for their age and place and of obeying the Manifestation's laws and commandments, and it also stated that "neither is acceptable without the other." In this way, the eternal Christian debate between faith and works was resolved in favor of both. Bahá'u'lláh continued by stating that anyone endowed with insight will

> readily recognize that the precepts laid down by God con-
> stitute the highest means for the maintenance of order in the
> world and the security of its peoples. He that turneth away
> from them is accounted among the abject and foolish. We,
> verily, have commanded you to refuse the dictates of your
> evil passions and corrupt desires, and not to transgress the
> bounds which the Pen of the Most High hath fixed, for these
> are the breath of life unto all created things.[25]

Utilizing mystic language alluding to the garment of Joseph (Qur. 12:94; Gen 37) he said that "From My laws the sweet-smelling savour of My garment can be smelled." But, he warned, "think not that We have revealed unto you a mere code of laws. Nay, rather, We have unsealed the choice Wine with the fingers of might and power."[26] Obedience of divine law was

---

[25] Bahá'u'lláh, The Kitáb-i-Aqdas, 19, 20.

[26] Bahá'u'lláh, The Kitáb-i-Aqdas, 20, 21.

not something that someone could claim to be exempt from because of spiritual status and achievement, as some Sufis had claimed in the past.

In the Aqdas, Bahá'u'lláh endorsed most of the positive laws and principles the Báb had stated in the Bayán and ignored or specifically abrogated the harsh laws of jihád in the same book. He defined the Bahá'í law of obligatory prayer but made it something one said privately and not in congregation, as was standard in Islam. Rather than giving the Bahá'ís one obligatory prayer, he gave them three, among which they could choose one to say each day. He endorsed the calendar the Báb promulgated and retained his law of fasting (no eating, drinking, or smoking from sunrise to sunset during the month of ʿAlá, which occurs during the nineteen days in March leading up to the spring equinox). Bahá'u'lláh established laws of marriage, divorce, and inheritance. All of these ordinances were expected by converts of Islamic background, who wanted a new sharíʿah to replace the old one. But Bahá'u'lláh banned monasticism and the establishment of clergy, forbade slavish imitation of others in favor of independent investigation of truth, forbade extreme asceticism, strongly discouraged celibacy, and encouraged marriage. He established only one communal ritual: the congregational prayer for the dead, which could be recited by anyone, male or female, young or old, on behalf of the group. He enjoined his followers to "recite ye the verses of God every morn and eventide" in order to strengthen their connection to the Word of God, and he called on them to repeat the Greatest Name of God, Alláh-u-Abhá (God is Most Glorious), 95 times a day in order to meditate on their Creator and on Bahá'u'lláh (whose title means the Glory of God).[27]

In place of clergy he ordained the establishment of "Houses of Justice," councils that provided a collective leadership. He limited legalism in various ways, first by refusing to circulate the Kitáb-i-Aqdas among the Bahá'ís for many years and then by offering relatively few answers to questions about the meaning of the laws, leaving it to the Bahá'ís to decide how to follow them. In this way the ordinances he established were something to obey "for the love of My beauty" and not out of a legal obligation.[28]

---

[27] Bahá'u'lláh, The Kitáb-i-Aqdas, 73. [28] Bahá'u'lláh, The Kitáb-i-Aqdas, 20.

Notably, Bahá'u'lláh did not create a weekly worship service, mass, or other weekly ritual for his community. Rather, he called on the Bahá'ís to gather together once every Bahá'í month (every nineteen days) for hospitality. Such gatherings could be small and informal and had no ritual associated with them, so they could be organized by anyone and could accommodate any local culture or circumstance. From this ordinance evolved the Bahá'í Nineteen-Day Feast, the regular Bahá'í community gathering. It begins with a period of worship, followed by discussion of community business, and concludes with hospitality. Feast assumed its current form in the early twentieth century and has no specific rituals associated with it.

Bahá'u'lláh also established holy days for his religion, a practice that developed further into the twentieth century. Eventually the Faith came to have nine holy days on which work was to be suspended: Bahá'í Naw-Rúz or New Year (the day of the spring equinox in late March); the first, ninth, and twelfth days of Bahá'u'lláh's declaration of his mission in the garden of Riḍván, the day the Báb declared himself to his first believer in 1844; the birthdays of the Báb and Bahá'u'lláh; and the days of their passings.[29] Thus eight of the nine holy days focus the believers on the lives of the two founding Manifestations. The calendar also has "intercalary days" (four of them in most years, five in a leap year); these are necessary because nineteen months of nineteen days each totals 361 days. These days are dedicated to celebration, service to others, and preparation for the Bahá'í Fast, which follows them.

---

[29] During years when Naw-Rúz (the first day of spring) occurs before sunset on March 21 in Tehran, Iran, the first, ninth, and twelfth days of Ridván fall on April 21, 29, and May 2; the Declaration of the Báb on May 24; the Martyrdom of the Báb on July 10; and the Ascension of Bahá'u'lláh on May 29. If Naw-Rúz occurs before sunset on March 20, the dates of all these holy days fall one day earlier in the Gregorian calendar. The Births of the Báb and Bahá'u'lláh are celebrated on the first and second days after the eighth new moon following the first day of spring. Two other holy days are the Day of the Covenant and the Ascension of ʿAbdu'l-Bahá, which fall on November 26 and 28 respectively when Naw-Rúz falls on March 21. The suspension of work is not required on those two days.

In addition, in the Aqdas Bahá'u'lláh forbade gambling and gossip. He banned the consumption of alcohol and opium, adding, "beware of using any substance that induceth sluggishness and torpor in the human temple and inflicteth harm upon the body."[30] He accepted the death penalty for two crimes only: premeditated murder and arson (presumably that causes death), though he allowed for life imprisonment as an alternative. He called for universal education, an essential if one wishes to create a community of strivers who lack clerical authorities and mystic experts. He insisted on kindness to animals. He began to elaborate on principles for world order, calling for the convocation of a summit of world leaders, the promulgation of international standards, and the selection of an international auxiliary language and script.

During Bahá'u'lláh's remaining two decades, the topics he discussed were diverse. He wrote more theological and philosophical treatises and defined additional principles for world order. In the Lawḥ-i-Maqṣúd he described human beings as the "supreme Talisman" but stated that "lack of a proper education hath . . . deprived him of that which he doth inherently possess. . . . Regard man as a mine rich in gems. Education can, alone, cause it to reveal its treasures, and enable mankind to benefit therefrom." In other writings, Bahá'u'lláh elaborated on this principle, explaining that "schools must first train the children in the principles of religion . . . but this in such a measure that it may not injure the children by resulting in ignorant fanaticism and bigotry." In addition to teaching "the oneness of God and the laws of God," "arts, crafts, and sciences uplift the world of being, and are conducive to its exaltation. Knowledge is as wings to man's life, and a ladder for his ascent. Its acquisition is incumbent on everyone." Thus true education has both a spiritual component and a secular or mundane one, both of which are conducive to individual transformation.[31]

Bahá'u'lláh elaborated on his principles of world order in the Lawḥ-i-Maqṣúd. He called on "all nations to appoint some men of understanding and erudition to convene a gathering and through joint deliberation choose one language from among the varied existing languages, or create a new

---

[30] Bahá'u'lláh, The Kitáb-i-Aqdas, 75.
[31] Universal House of Justice, *A Compilation of Compilations*, 248–9.

one, to be taught to the children in all the schools of the world. . . . When this is achieved, to whatsoever city a man may journey, it shall be as if he were entering his own home."[32]

In the Lawḥ-i-Maqṣúd, Bahá'u'lláh wrote that "one indeed is a man who, today, dedicateth himself to the service of the entire human race. . . . Blessed and happy is he that ariseth to promote the best interests of the peoples and kindreds of the earth. . . . It is not for him to pride himself who loves his country, but rather for him who loveth the whole world. The earth is but one country, and mankind its citizens."[33] This passage set the Bahá'í community on a very internationalist, even cosmopolitan, path, encouraging such things as settling in other countries and marrying people from other cultures. It also occasionally caused critics to accuse Bahá'ís wrongly of being indifferent to their own countries.

In a tablet to a prominent Zoroastrian leader, Bahá'u'lláh called on everyone to be "anxiously concerned with the needs of the age ye live in, and centre your deliberations on its exigencies and requirements," because "every age hath its own problem." In another tablet he added that "all men have been created to carry forward an ever-advancing civilization." Both passages established the important principle of practical and active engagement in the world as one of the dimensions of human development and ultimately of spiritual transformation.[34]

In the short obligatory prayer Bahá'u'lláh defined the individual's purpose as "to know Thee [God] and worship Thee."[35] Here, Bahá'u'lláh established a second dimension of the spiritual striver's transformation: a vertical one involving one's growing relationship with God. To reinforce both the vertical dimension and the horizontal dimension of one's involvement in the life of others and of society, Bahá'u'lláh composed scores – perhaps hundreds – of

[32] Bahá'u'lláh, *Tablets of Bahá'u'lláh Revealed After the Kitáb-i-Aqdas*, 165–6.

[33] Bahá'u'lláh, *Tablets of Bahá'u'lláh Revealed After the Kitáb-i-Aqdas*, 167.

[34] Bahá'u'lláh, *The Tabernacle of Unity*, 8; *Gleanings from the Writings of Bahá'u'lláh*, 214.

[35] Bahá'u'lláh, *Bahá'í Prayers*, 4. Bahá'u'lláh revealed three obligatory prayers, and a Bahá'í chooses which one to say each day.

prayers to say in one's daily devotions. These were later compiled together, translated, and published in prayer books.

At a time when Iranian women were veiled and often confined to the home, and rarely were taught to read, Bahá'u'lláh said, "Praised be unto God, the Pen of the Most High hath lifted distinctions from between His servants and handmaidens and, through His consummate favours and all-encompassing mercy, hath conferred upon all a station and rank on the same plane."[36] He said that all should have training in order to pursue a profession, a principle that included women, thereby implying the right of women to be educated and to work. He abolished arranged marriage and stated that each person should choose his or her spouse. Together, these teachings imply the equality of men and women, even though Bahá'u'lláh did not state it that way (possibly because that phrase did not exist or was not current in the Arabic and Persian of his day).

In a late work, the Lawḥ-i-Bishárát or "Tablet of Glad-Tidings," Bahá'u'lláh offered a series of principles for creating a world civilization. Some he had already mentioned, such as the oneness of humanity and the need for an international language. He reiterated that "the law of holy war [jihád] hath been blotted out from the Book." He emphasized that work, performed in service of others, is a form of worship: "It is enjoined upon every one of you to engage in some form of occupation, such as crafts, trades and the like. We have graciously exalted your engagement in such work to the rank of worship unto God, the True One. . . . Waste not your time in idleness and sloth. Occupy yourselves with that which profiteth yourselves and others."[37]

In his last major work, Epistle to the Son of the Wolf, a compilation of and commentary on some of the choicest passages from his literary corpus, Bahá'u'lláh uses jihád in a wholly non-violent and spiritual sense:

> O peoples of the earth! Haste ye to do the pleasure of God, and war ye valiantly, as it behooveth you to war (jáhidú

---

[36] Bahá'u'lláh, quoted in *Women: Extracts from the Writings of Bahá'u'lláh, 'Abdu'l-Bahá, Shoghi Effendi and the Universal House of Justice*, 2.

[37] Bahá'u'lláh, *Tablets of Bahá'u'lláh Revealed After the Kitáb-i-Aqdas*, 21, 25.

ḥaqqa'l-jihád), for the sake of proclaiming His resistless and immovable Cause. We have decreed that war (al-jihád) shall be waged in the path of God with the armies of wisdom and utterance, and of a goodly character and praiseworthy deeds.[38]

Later in that work, Bahá'u'lláh expresses

the hope that He [God] may graciously assist the . . . kings of the earth . . . to establish the Lesser Peace. . . . It is their duty to convene an all-inclusive assembly, which either they themselves or their ministers will attend, and to enforce whatever measures are required to establish unity and concord amongst men. They must put away the weapons of war, and turn to the instruments of universal reconstruction. Should one king rise up against another, all the other kings must arise to deter him. Arms and armaments will, then, be no more needed beyond that which is necessary to ensure the internal security of their respective countries.[39]

Here, Bahá'u'lláh mentions the "lesser peace," a peace that is to be established by the nations themselves. He recognizes that before it is attained, nations might attack each other, and that a united effort, potentially including warfare, is justifiable to prevent them. Thus the Bahá'í Faith is not pacifist; it recognizes the possible need for war as a last resort to maintain peace.

5 Other References about Violence and Non-violence

It is clear from the above summary of Bahá'u'lláh's writings that he sought to define a peaceful, inclusive, just, non-violent human civilization. But in many places, Bahá'u'lláh elaborated on the abolition of the "principle of the

---

[38] Bahá'u'lláh, Epistle to the Son of the Wolf, 24. I am indebted to Omid Ghaemmaghami for pointing out this passage to me and supplying the Arabic text.

[39] Bahá'u'lláh, Epistle to the Son of the Wolf, 30–1.

sword" in order to make the non-violent nature of his teachings absolutely clear:

> By "rendering assistance unto God," then, it is not meant that any soul should fight or contend with another ... rendering assistance unto God, in this day, doth not and shall never consist in contending or disputing with any soul; nay rather, what is preferable in the sight of God is that the cities of men's hearts, which are ruled by the hosts of self and passion, should be subdued by the sword of utterance, of wisdom and of understanding. Thus, whoso seeketh to assist God must, before all else, conquer, with the sword of inner meaning and explanation, the city of his own heart and guard it from the remembrance of all save God, and only then set out to subdue the cities of the hearts of others.
>
> Such is the true meaning of rendering assistance unto God. Sedition hath never been pleasing unto God, nor were the acts committed in the past by certain foolish ones acceptable in His sight. Know ye that to be killed in the path of His good pleasure is better for you than to kill. The beloved of the Lord must, in this day, behave in such wise amidst His servants that they may by their very deeds and actions guide all men unto the paradise of the All-Glorious.[40]

Note particularly his stress that is better to be killed than to kill. This set the Bahá'í community on a non-violent path, even to the extent that the defensive jihád practiced by the Bábís was forbidden. The result was a dramatic de-escalation of violence against the Bahá'í community. Whenever a Bahá'í was martyred for his faith, the community took the moral high ground by appealing to the authorities, the public, and the press, which generally prevented any immediate additional acts of violence and sometimes even resulted in punishment of the perpetrators. Bahá'ís are allowed to protect themselves from robbers, as circumstances permit, and are allowed to serve in the military, but they cannot use violence to protect themselves or their religious community from people who seek to murder them for their faith.[41]

The Bahá'í attitude toward martyrdom was also an important factor in limiting the effectiveness of persecution. Shí'í Islam allowed the practice of dissimulation or denying one's faith under duress. Bahá'u'lláh modified this principle by forbidding an outright lie about one's beliefs (though the use of "wisdom" in what one said about one's faith was permissible). If commanded to renounce one's faith or be killed, Shi'ites could renounce, but Bahá'ís could not; martyrdom for the truth was spiritually preferable and praised as the highest sacrifice one could make. As a result, it was not possible to round up thousands of Bahá'ís, force them to renounce their faith, convert them to Islam, and thereby destroy the community. The martyrdoms of a few protected the many and kept the community alive and united.

There was one notable exception to the Bahá'í practice of non-violent resistance to persecution. About 1872, seven companions of Bahá'u'lláh, infuriated by the trouble and persecution that three men were causing him, murdered the three in cold blood. Bahá'u'lláh himself had warned them repeatedly against any effort to retaliate against the men and was deeply grieved by the incident.[42]

During his thirty years of ministry, Bahá'u'lláh had provided guidance about almost every imaginable topic, from the raising of babies to the charging of interest, from the use of music to the importance of agriculture. The theme behind many of the teachings is the oneness of humanity and the ethical imperative of bringing about the unity of the human family. Such a theme, obviously, has significant implications regarding violence and non-violence.

---

[41] Letter of the Universal House of Justice to the National Spiritual Assembly of the Bahá'ís of Honduras, quoting 'Abdu'l-Bahá, in *Lights of Guidance*, 117.

[42] H. M. Balyuzi, *Bahá'u'lláh: The King of Glory* (Oxford: George Ronald, 1980), 325–7.

Bahá'u'lláh also clearly stated in several tablets that ʿAbbás Effendi (1844–1921), his oldest son, was to be his successor, that all Bahá'ís had to turn to him, and that he was authorized to interpret Bahá'u'lláh's teachings. As a result, when Bahá'u'lláh passed in 1892, the leadership transition was relatively smooth. ʿAbbás took the title of ʿAbdu'l-Bahá, "the servant of Bahá," to emphasize his complete subservience to the religion of his father. He sought, through his talks, writings, and life, to demonstrate that the highest station anyone could achieve was the station of service to others.

6 Bahá'u'lláh and ʿAbdu'l-Bahá about Oneness and Unity

ʿAbdu'l-Bahá once commented that the purpose of Bahá'u'lláh's life and the reason he endured enormous hardships was to ensure that "the oneness of humankind become a reality, strife and warfare cease and peace and tranquility be realized by all." Bahá'u'lláh once noted that "no two men can be found who may be said to be outwardly and inwardly united."[43] He defined the basis of his religion on the theological principle of the oneness of humanity – that all humans are from the same stock – and the consequent ethical principle of unity. In his ethical and moral piece titled The Hidden Words, composed about 1860, Bahá'u'lláh, speaking in the voice of God, says:

> [K]now ye not why We created you all from the same dust? That no one should exalt himself over the other. Ponder at all times in your hearts how ye were created. Since We have created you all from one same substance it is incumbent on you to be even as one soul, to walk with the same feet, eat with the same mouth and dwell in the same land, that from your inmost being, by your deeds and actions, the signs of oneness and the essence of detachment may be made manifest.[44]

[43] ʿAbdu'l-Bahá, *Bahá'í World Faith*, 230; Bahá'u'lláh, *Tablets of Bahá'u'lláh Revealed After the Kitáb-i-Aqdas*, 161–2.

[44] Bahá'u'lláh, Arabic Hidden Words, no. 68.

Here, Bahá'u'lláh clearly ties oneness and unity together. While the oneness of humanity is a biological fact, unity is something that must be achieved. It can be conceived as a process that starts at a practical level, but it should progress toward a spiritual state of unity. Bahá'u'lláh offers a pragmatic metaphor for the practical form of unity: "be ye as the fingers of one hand, the members of one body."[45] A hand needs fingers in order to function; a body depends on the complementary efforts of its organs. Through cooperation, groups of people can build trust and pursue efforts of increasing difficulty and complexity. Efforts to work together are emphasized and highly praised in the Bahá'í writings, which state "verily, God loveth those who are working in His path in groups, for they are a solid foundation."[46]

But beyond the practical steps to collaborate is a deeper form of spiritual unity. This idealized form of unity is expressed in the metaphor that the Bahá'ís should be "one soul in many bodies."[47] 'Abdu'l-Bahá describes it in these words:

> Another unity is the spiritual unity which emanates from the breaths of the Holy Spirit. . . . Human unity or solidarity may be likened to the body, whereas unity from the breaths of the Holy Spirit is the spirit animating the body. This is a perfect unity. It creates such a condition in mankind that each one will make sacrifices for the other, and the utmost desire will be to forfeit life and all that pertains to it in behalf of another's good. This is the unity which existed among the disciples of Jesus Christ and bound together the Prophets and holy Souls of the past. It is the unity which through the influence of the divine spirit is permeating the Bahá'ís so that each offers his life for the other and strives with all sincerity to attain his good pleasure.[48]

[45] Bahá'u'lláh, *Kitáb-i-Aqdas*, para. 58.
[46] 'Abdu'l-Bahá, in *Bahá'í World Faith*, 401.
[47] 'Abdu'l-Bahá, quoted in Shoghi Effendi, *The Lights of Divine Guidance*, vol. 2, 50.
[48] 'Abdu'l-Bahá, *Promulgation of Universal Peace*, 191–2.

Metaphors of oneness abound in Bahá'u'lláh's writings; human beings are the leaves of one branch, the flowers of one garden, the waves of one sea. By abolishing the notion of ritual purity and impurity, Bahá'u'lláh eliminated the notion that people can be unclean. By abolishing the notion of unclean food, Bahá'u'lláh allowed Bahá'ís to eat any food with anyone.

Bahá'u'lláh challenged many of the other distinctions that separate people. He abolished slavery. He commanded universal literacy so that all could read and study the word of God and could contribute to an ever-advancing civilization. He called on the Bahá'ís to reach out to people of other ethnic and religious backgrounds and attract them to the Bahá'í community so that it was diverse and inclusive. These principles implied a rejection of racism and an emphasis on the equality of all peoples.

Bahá'u'lláh and ʿAbdu'l-Bahá disseminated the Bahá'í teachings through meetings with visiting pilgrims, via teachers they sent to parts of Asia and Africa, and through extensive correspondence with thousands of followers. As a result, in the late nineteenth and early twentieth centuries, thousands of Iranians converted, including significant numbers of Iranian Jews and Zoroastrians, who were oppressed minorities in Persian society. Bahá'í communities sprang up in Egypt, Lebanon, Syria, Iraq, Turkey, Russian Central Asia, India, Burma, and even the Dutch East Indies, though the converts there could not be consolidated. Middle Eastern Christians and possibly Burmese Buddhists converted in small numbers starting in the 1880s and 1890s, further diversifying the community. Just weeks before his passing in May 1892, Bahá'u'lláh authorized the trip of Ibrahim Kheiralla and Anton Haddad, two Bahá'ís of Lebanese Christian background, to Europe and the United States. By 1900 Kheiralla had brought about 1,500 Americans, mostly of white Protestant middle-class background, into the Faith.

With the growth of a Bahá'í community in the United States, the issue of racial diversity arose. As early as 1898, an African-American man, Robert Turner – the butler of a white Bahá'í, Phoebe Hearst – became a Bahá'í in California. An African-American woman, Olive Jackson, joined the Bahá'í Faith in New York City in 1899.[49] But the first Bahá'í community that faced

[49] Stockman, *The Bahá'í Faith in America*, vol. 1, 139–40, 126–7.

the issue of racial integration was Washington, DC, where Pauline Hannen, a white southerner, realized the importance of reaching African Americans with the Bahá'í Faith. She had been born in 1874 and raised in Wilmington, North Carolina; she became a Bahá'í in 1902. She was inspired by the passage of the Hidden Words already quoted, "Know ye not why We created you all from the same dust? That no one should exalt himself over another." One November day about 1904, while walking down the street, she saw an African-American woman trudging toward her, arms loaded with bundles of groceries. She could not see that her shoes were untied and was unable to put her bundles down in the snow. Spontaneously, Pauline stopped the woman and tied her shoes, to the astonishment of the woman and the shock of the white people present. It was Pauline's turning point. She, her husband, and her two sisters decided they had to teach the Bahá'í Faith to the African Americans they knew on a basis of equality, starting with their washerwoman and seamstress.[50]

It took more than one passage from Bahá'u'lláh's writings, however, to bring about a racially integrated community. 'Abdu'l-Bahá was anxious to see a unified Bahá'í community be established in Washington. He wrote many letters to the city's white and black Bahá'ís explaining the importance of demonstrating the oneness of humanity in the Bahá'í communities, and he even endorsed interracial marriage as an ideal expression of such oneness. When Louis Gregory, an African-American lawyer who became a Bahá'í through the Hannens in 1909, went on pilgrimage to meet 'Abdu'l-Bahá in 1911, they spent hours discussing the Bahá'í principle of equality and the situation of African Americans, and 'Abdu'l-Bahá urged Gregory to "work for unity and harmony between the races."[51]

In 1912, 'Abdu'l-Bahá visited the United States for eight months and spent as much time as he could meeting African Americans. He spoke to 1,600 at Howard University, to perhaps 2,000 at Metropolitan African Methodist Episcopal Church in Washington, and to 750 at the fourth annual

---

[50] Robert Stockman, *The Bahá'í Faith in America*, *vol. 1: Origins, 1892–1900*, 126–7, 139–40; Arabic Hidden Words, no. 68; *The Bahá'í Faith in America*, *vol. 2: Early Expansion, 1900–1912*, 225.

[51] 'Abdu'l-Bahá, quoted in Gayle Morrison, *To Move the World*, 46.

conference of the National Association for the Advancement of Colored People (NAACP) in Chicago. The latter talk prompted W. E. B. Du Bois to feature ʿAbdu'l-Bahá as "man of the month" in the May 1912 issue of *The Crisis* and to reprint his NAACP and Hull House speeches in the June issue.[52] Eventually Robert Abbott, the publisher of the *Chicago Defender*, the country's leading African-American newspaper, became a Bahá'í. Ida Wells, a Chicago black activist, also briefly became a Bahá'í.

ʿAbdu'l-Bahá arranged small, private meetings with African Americans, such as a Sunday meeting with the black servants of the rich white vacationers in Dublin, New Hampshire, which had to be held in a boathouse because nothing else would be provided. He rented houses during his travels rather than residing in hotels, partly because he could entertain anyone in a private residence. He asked a Japanese-American Bahá'í to join his entourage for his trip to California, where prejudice against East Asians was high, and he spoke to the Japanese Independent Church in Oakland. His efforts were not confined to ethnic differences; when a poor white Bahá'í named Fred Mortensen arrived in Maine to see ʿAbdu'l-Bahá, having ridden on the tops and under trains because he couldn't afford a ticket, ʿAbdu'l-Bahá sat him in the place of honor on his right in a dinner for otherwise middle-class American Bahá'ís. He made a similar gesture by asking Louis Gregory to stay for a formal dinner at the home of the Persian chargé d'affaires in Washington and seating the black lawyer at his right hand.[53]

But undoubtedly his most important effort to demonstrate the oneness of humanity was his decision to invite Louisa Mathew – an English woman who had been on pilgrimage at the same time as Louis Gregory – to travel to the United States with him. When Louis and Louisa had visited him in Egypt, he must have seen a potential relationship. In America, several times ʿAbdu'l-Bahá hinted that he thought Louis and Louisa should consider marriage, an idea that shocked and frightened Louis when he finally understood ʿAbdu'l-Bahá's intention. But the two got to know each other over a six-month period and married in September 1912, the first interracial

[52] Stockman, *ʿAbdu'l-Bahá in America*, 97, 101, 110, 114.

[53] Stockman, *ʿAbdu'l-Bahá in America*, 223–4, 259, 286–8, 244, 100.

marriage in the American Bahá'í community.[54] The marriage was a shock for many American Bahá'ís, whose notion of equality and unity was far more theoretical than actual. But it moved the American Bahá'í community on a path toward racial inclusion that, with many ups and downs, has continued to this day.

'Abdu'l-Bahá also continued his father's efforts to diversify the Bahá'í community worldwide. He sent Americans to Iran and Iranians to the United States to teach the Faith, as well as joint teams of Iranians and Americans to India. He encouraged the American Bahá'ís to support Iranian Bahá'í schools with books and money, and he encouraged Iranian Bahá'ís to donate to the construction of the first Bahá'í House of Worship in North America. He encouraged four American Bahá'í women – two physicians and two nurses – to settle in Iran between 1909 and 1911, to help the Bahá'ís build a clinic and a school for girls, and inevitably to expose the Iranian Bahá'ís to the Western understanding of equality of men and women. He encouraged regular correspondence between groups of American and Iranian Bahá'í women. He wrote to the Iranian Bahá'í women and counseled patience with the pace of change, while actively encouraging their advancement. He encouraged the Zoroastrian and Jewish Bahá'ís to mix and mingle with their coreligionists of Shí'í background, which eliminated the alienation and distrust they originally felt for each other and gradually resulted in intermarriage and the fusion of the three groups into one community. He oversaw the first Hindu and Sikh conversions to the Faith in India. He visited Bahá'í communities in Egypt, England, France, Germany, and Canada and encouraged American Bahá'ís to take the Faith to Japan, Korea, China, Australia, New Zealand, and South America. He often asked Bahá'ís embarking on international trips to come meet him first, so he could advise them personally. While none of these efforts can be characterized as maintaining non-violence, they were carefully planned to bring together people with very different cultural expectations in ways that minimized friction and disagreements. The strategy was clear: to build a peaceful and non-violent world civilization, one first had to build a diverse and representative religious community.

[54] Morrison, *To Move the World*, 63–72.

'Abdu'l-Bahá was also an astute observer of the issues of Western civilization and commented frequently about solutions to its problems. When asked about the problem of strikes, he started by observing that "the root cause of these difficulties lie in the law of nature that governs present day civilization," in other words the Darwinian notion of survival of the fittest. While a Darwinian struggle brought balance and ecological diversity to nature, social Darwinism simply allowed the ambitious and greedy to amass power and wealth while impoverishing and disempowering the majority. A Marxian approach – "complete equality in wealth, power, commerce, agriculture, and industry" – also would not work, because it would produce "chaos and disorder, disrupt livelihoods, provoke universal discontent, and undermine the orderly affairs of the community." Instead, 'Abdu'l-Bahá, like the progressives of his day, advocated "the enactment of such laws and regulations as would prevent the unwarranted concentration of wealth in the hands of the few and satisfy the essential needs of the many." A graduated income tax, profit sharing, retirement pensions, unemployment assistance, a welfare system for the disabled and needy, and a publicly supported health-care system were among the measures he advocated.[55]

In his hundreds of talks in North America and Europe, 'Abdu'l-Bahá honed a presentation that explored a series of principles. Independent investigation of truth was one of the most important topics he addressed. He stressed the importance of rational study of all phenomena, including religion, praised Plato and Aristotle highly, and called on people not to follow the faiths of their ancestors blindly but to explore them, let go of minor differences and outmoded rituals, and stress their commonalities with other traditions. As such, he was developing further Bahá'u'lláh's description of the true seeker using language suitable for his Western audience.

A related principle he often spoke about was the harmony of religion with science: "if belief and teaching are opposed to the analysis of reason and principles of science, they are not worthy of acceptance."[56] At the time

---

[55] 'Abdu'l-Bahá, *Some Answered Questions*, 315–17; Zarqání, *Maḥmud's Diary*, 206–7.

[56] 'Abdu'l-Bahá, *The Promulgation of Universal Peace*, 434.

it was common for the representatives of the different faiths to emphasize the harmony of religion with science and reason – both the Buddhist Dharmapala and the Hindu Swami Vivekananda did it in their talks in the west – but for ʿAbduʾl-Bahá the principle of the harmony of science and religion was an extension of the Baháʾí principle that reality is one and that it can be explored through both natural phenomena and spiritual efforts, as well as being an extension of the principle of independent investigation of reality.

7 Building Unity through Organization

One cannot maintain a non-violent community without a mechanism to resolve disputes. Baháʾuʾlláh tackled this problem through the type of religious organization he created and by defining the nature and extent of its authority. By abolishing the institution of clergy, he created a community of equal adults and mandated the establishment of coordinating councils at the local level (called local Spiritual Assemblies) and the international level (termed the Universal House of Justice). ʿAbduʾl-Bahá added that there were to be national coordinating councils (termed National Spiritual Assemblies) as well and said that all the councils were to be chosen via election. In Iran, the elections involved no nominations or campaigning. Shoghi Effendi Rabbani (1897–1957), ʿAbduʾl-Bahá's grandson and successor as Guardian of the Baháʾí Faith, explained that the elections should involve no prior mention of names by anyone at all.[57] Individuals should gather, pray together, read and contemplate some statements about the qualities of character and experience one should consider, and vote without any outside influence.

Shoghi Effendi's secretary explained the reason for this procedure:

[57] ʿAbduʾl-Bahá appointed Shoghi Effendi his successor in his Will and Testament. He specified that Shoghi Effendi was infallible in matters related to interpretation of the Baháʾí scriptures and protection of the Faith and enjoined all Baháʾís to obey him. In Shoghi Effendi's thirty-six-year ministry (1921–57) he wrote over 34,000 unique works, mostly letters, totaling over 5 million words. He wrote in Arabic, Persian, English, and, to a much lesser degree, French.

As to the practice of nomination in Bahá'í elections, this the Guardian firmly believes to be in fundamental disaccord with the spirit which should animate and direct all elections held by the Bahá'ís, be they of a local or national character and importance. It is, indeed, the absence of such a practice that constitutes the distinguishing feature and the marked superiority of the Bahá'í electoral methods over those commonly associated with political parties and factions. The practice of nomination being thus contrary to the spirit of Bahá'í Administration should be totally discarded by all the friends. For otherwise the freedom of the Bahá'í elector in choosing the members of any Bahá'í assembly will be seriously endangered, leaving the way open for the domination of personalities. Not only that; but the mere act of nomination – leads eventually to the formation of parties – a thing which is totally alien to the spirit of the Cause.

In addition to these serious dangers, the practice of nomination has the great disadvantage of killing in the believer the spirit of initiative, and of self-development. Bahá'í electoral procedures and methods have, indeed, for one of their essential purposes the development in every believer of the spirit of responsibility. By emphasizing the necessity of maintaining his full freedom in the elections, they make it incumbent upon him to become an active and well-informed member of the Bahá'í community in which he lives. To be able to make a wise choice at the election time, it is necessary for him to be in close and continued contact with all local activities, be they teaching, administrative or otherwise, and to fully and whole-heartedly participate in the affairs of the local as well as national committees and assemblies in his country. It is only in this way that a believer can develop a true social consciousness and acquire a true sense of responsibility in matters affecting the interests of the Cause. Bahá'í community life thus makes it a duty for every loyal and faithful believer to become an intelligent, well-informed and responsible elector, and also gives him the opportunity of raising himself to such a station. And since the practice of nomination hinders the development of such qualities in the believer, and in addition leads to corruption and partisanship, it has to be entirely discarded in all Bahá'í elections.[58]

The text provides a number of reasons to reject the practice of nomination: it leads to the domination of personalities, the formation of parties and partisanship, fosters dependence of the voter on others, and kills the spirit of initiative and self development. A crucial point is that the Bahá'í approach to unity is not compatible with partisanship, which creates ill will, strife, cynicism, a dysfunctional political process, and distrust of the government and which can lead to violent clashes and assassinations. In short, from a Bahá'í point of view, structural violence is built into the nature of partisanship. For this reason, Bahá'ís do not join or support political parties, and they seek to do their public discourse in a nonpartisan or bipartisan manner.

Within the Bahá'í community, elections are not casual, secular acts; they are a sacred process that begins with prayers and the recitation of passages from Bahá'í scripture. In a religion almost entirely lacking communal ritual, the election constitutes a central community practice; it could almost be compared to Christian communion. Shoghi Effendi emphasized one should prepare spiritually before voting and strive for a spirit of humility and detachment in casting one's vote. He advised that one should vote for "those who can best combine the necessary qualities of unquestioned loyalty, of selfless devotion, of a well-trained mind, of recognized ability and mature experience."[59] Because Bahá'í elections occur without any nominations or campaigning, there can be no voter manipulation, exaggerating one's capabilities, minimizing the abilities of others, promised actions, or party platforms. With no promises to keep, the elected members are free to consider matters on their merits, rather than whether they reinforce or weaken one's campaign positions. One result is that it is extremely difficult to define what

[58] Shoghi Effendi, *The Light of Divine Guidance v. I*, 67–8.
[59] Shoghi Effendi, *Bahá'í Administration*, 88.

a "liberal" or a "conservative" Bahá'í would be, because there are few if any controversial subjects within the community. The entire process increases confidence in one's institutions rather than undermining them.

Local Bahá'í elections occur annually on the first day of Riḍván, the holiest Bahá'í holy day, marking the day Bahá'u'lláh declared his mission in the Riḍván garden in Baghdad.[60] All members of a local Bahá'í community – which is generally defined based on the borders of local civic jurisdictions, such as a city or county – who are over the age of twenty-one are eligible to vote and to be elected. The result is the nine-member local Spiritual Assembly of that place. If a tie occurs for the ninth position on the Assembly and one of the persons voted for is a minority, the minority member is automatically elected; otherwise, a vote to break the tie is held. The Assembly coordinates Bahá'í activities in that locality, oversees Bahá'í marriages, assists with Bahá'í funerals, enrolls new members of the community, counsels people with personal difficulties (often through a counseling committee in large communities), maintains a fund, and owns any community property, such as a Bahá'í center. In many areas of the world, once a year all the members of all the local Spiritual Assemblies in a region vote to elect a nine-member Regional Bahá'í Council, which coordinates Bahá'í activity at the regional level.

Once a year, also, National Spiritual Assemblies are elected. Each country is divided into electoral districts, each of which normally elects one delegate by the same process of prayer and silent voting, and the delegates gather in April or May to elect the National Spiritual Assembly. Once every five years, all the members of all the National Spiritual Assemblies worldwide – some 170 Assemblies, with nine members each – gather in Haifa, Israel, to elect the nine-member Universal House of Justice. All the elections worldwide follow the same universal procedure, with one exception: while women can and are elected to local and national Spiritual Assemblies, they are not eligible to be elected to the Universal House of Justice. According to the Will and Testament of 'Abdu'l-Bahá, the Universal House of Justice is infallible to guide and

---

[60] This falls thirty-one days after the spring equinox, usually either April 20 or 21.

protect the Bahá'í community and to legislate on matters not covered by the writings of the Báb, Bahá'u'lláh, 'Abdu'l-Bahá, and Shoghi Effendi.[61]

While coordination of Bahá'í activities is performed by elected councils, there is a role for individual advisors. The Universal House of Justice appoints, to a five-year term, Counselors (currently, eighty-one worldwide) who advise and encourage Bahá'ís and their institutions. They in turn appoint Auxiliary Board members (currently, 990 worldwide), who appoint assistants at the local level. These individuals have no clerical role in the Bahá'í Faith; they have no special privileges, no station apart from that of the believer, and no authority by virtue of their appointment. They are uniquely positioned to inform the Universal House of Justice of developments at the grassroots and in turn to convey to the local Bahá'ís the priorities and plans established by the Universal House of Justice.

Spiritual unity is the ultimate goal of many Baha'i efforts. Almost every Bahá'í event starts with prayers by Bahá'u'lláh, the Báb, or 'Abdu'l-Bahá in order to establish a rarefied atmosphere and invoke a spiritual dynamic that allows the gathering to achieve its true purpose.[62] The creation of spiritual unity is a principal purpose of the Nineteen-Day Feast, the monthly Bahá'í community gathering for worship, consultation, and socializing.[63]

[61] Because the Universal House of Justice can make decisions by a majority vote (five out of nine members), there is no notion that the individual members of the Universal House of Justice are infallible. On the contrary, their station is that of an ordinary believer. It is not known why women cannot serve on the Universal House of Justice.

[62] When Bahá'ís pray they almost always use written prayers revealed by Bahá'u'lláh and 'Abdu'l-Bahá, not prayers composed by themselves or by other Bahá'ís. In this way Bahá'í prayer is an act of reconnection to revelation and to scripture.

[63] Bahá'ís do not normally conduct worship on a weekly basis, as do mosques, churches, and synagogues. The Nineteen-Day Feast occurs once every Bahá'í month (which last nineteen days, there being nineteen Bahá'í months in a solar year). It was initiated by Bahá'u'lláh, developed by 'Abdu'l-Bahá (who made it a Bahá'í community event every Bahá'í month involving worship and social portions), and refined by Shoghi Effendi (who added the portion for consultation on community business).

'Abdu'l-Bahá composed a prayer to use at the start of meetings of Spiritual Assemblies that asks that "our thoughts, our views, our feelings may become as one reality, manifesting the spirit of union throughout the world,"[64] a prayer designed to foster spiritual unity. Spiritual unity is also a goal of Bahá'í conventions, where spiritual assemblies are elected. Many Bahá'í prayer books contain a section titled "meetings" filled with prayers that seek, in their poetic language and the divine power they invoke, to create spiritual unity.

8 The Authority of Bahá'í Institutions: The Covenant

As already noted, Bahá'í institutions are backed up by a very strong claim of authority. Bahá'u'lláh made clear and definite claims in writing to be the mouthpiece of God for this day, the Manifestation for a new era of human civilization, the Promised One of all the world's religions, and the return of Christ. These claims were expressed through a remarkable life, an enormous capacity to suffer for his claim – he was exiled four times, was imprisoned twice, was beaten, was poisoned, and lost all his possessions – and a vast and singularly unique literary legacy that far exceeds the Bible in length. Among his writings were those appointing 'Abdu'l-Bahá his successor, declaring him "the Mystery of God" and granting 'Abdu'l-Bahá infallible authority over the community and the power of infallible interpretation of Bahá'u'lláh's intent. 'Abdu'l-Bahá, in turn, in his Will and Testament conferred the power of infallible interpretation on Shoghi Effendi as the first (and only) Guardian and the power of infallible legislation on the Universal House of Justice, as his twin successors.

Because the documentation of the transfer of authority is clear, the Bahá'í Faith has essentially no sects. Historically, a dozen efforts have been made to split the Bahá'í community: after Bahá'u'lláh's death, a small number rejected 'Abdu'l-Bahá; after 'Abdu'l-Bahá's passing a small number rejected Shoghi Effendi; and after Shoghi Effendi's unexpected passing in 1957 a small number rejected the end of the Guardianship and the election of the Universal House of Justice (which occurred in 1963). In each case a charismatic individual

---

[64] 'Abdu'l-Bahá, in *Bahá'í Prayers*, 138.

made some sort of claim to authority, the vast majority of Bahá'ís rejected it based on the written documents defining successorship, a small number of people (usually less than 100) followed the claimant, and over a few decades the competitive movement withered away. Today the Bahá'í community has some 5 million members; the Orthodox Bahá'í Faith perhaps 100; and the Bahá'ís Under the Provision of the Covenant several dozen, who are in turn divided into two sects, one of which appears to be inactive.

Bahá'ís term this clear succession the Covenant of Bahá'u'lláh and the small number who have rejected it as Covenant breakers. Covenant breaking is one area where anxiety, high emotion, and potential conflict can be found in the Bahá'í community. Because the Covenant is so clear, it takes an unusual personality for someone to attempt a schism, and those who join the splinter group often have had an upsetting personal experience in the Bahá'í community. The splinter group's message usually focuses on the reasons they split from the Bahá'í community, and thus it is not attractive to non-Bahá'ís. Bahá'ís are told not to associate with the group, thereby denying the group any opportunity to recruit members. Consequently, most groups are active for about a generation and fade away as the children of the original Covenant breakers age. If any contact with the group or its members is necessary, it is generally handled by the Counselors or Auxiliary Board members. In this manner, the unity of the Bahá'í community is maintained peacefully.

9 Consultation

Bahá'u'lláh emphasized a process of decision-making called consultation (*shurá* in Arabic), and he tied it closely to the capacities of the spiritually striving believer:

> Every word is endowed with a spirit, therefore the speaker or expounder should carefully deliver his words at the appropriate time and place, for the impression which each word maketh is clearly evident and perceptible. The Great Being saith: One word may be likened unto fire, another unto light, and the influence which both exert is manifest in

the world. Therefore an enlightened man of wisdom should primarily speak with words as mild as milk, that the children of men may be nurtured and edified thereby and may attain the ultimate goal of human existence which is the station of true understanding and nobility. And likewise He saith: One word is like unto springtime causing the tender saplings of the rose-garden of knowledge to become verdant and flourishing, while another word is even as a deadly poison. It behoveth a prudent man of wisdom to speak with utmost leniency and forbearance so that the sweetness of his words may induce everyone to attain that which befitteth man's station.[65]

It is an ideal characteristic of a striving believer to know how to speak to others lovingly and persuasively; furthermore, learning how to communicate in a consultative fashion is an important means for becoming further transformed. Bahá'u'lláh noted that "in all things it is necessary to consult." 'Abdu'l-Bahá provided an additional list of spiritual virtues a believer should develop: "the prime requisites for them that take counsel together are purity of motive, radiance of spirit, detachment from all save God, attraction to His Divine Fragrances, humility and lowliness amongst His loved ones, patience and long-suffering in difficulties and servitude to His exalted threshold."[66] The purpose of consultation is to arrive at the truth through ascertaining the facts, listening, sharing, mutual respect, detachment from one's own opinions, and a prayerful attitude. People must express themselves frankly, on the one hand, and not take offense on the other. Because it is the etiquette of expression that a spiritually striving person is supposed to exercise, it is very different from the parliamentary process that most legislative bodies use. When used by Bahá'í Spiritual Assemblies, consultation does not include Robert's Rules of Order.

---

[65] Bahá'u'lláh, *Tablets of* Bahá'u'lláh *Revealed After the Kitáb-i-Aqdas*, 172–3.
[66] Bahá'u'lláh, in *Consultation: A Compilation*, 3; 'Abdu'l-Bahá, in *Consultation: A Compilation*, 5.

While the purpose of consultation is unity in truth, unanimity is not always possible. If consensus cannot be reached, a majority vote is acceptable, but if a majority decision proves necessary, there is no minority report, and those who disagree with the decision are bound to follow it. If they were to oppose the decision and the decision were to fail, it would be impossible to know whether the failure was caused by a poor decision or by opposition. Thus a decision must be supported and carried out in order to be sure it was either right or wrong. 'Abdu'l-Bahá even says in one passage that "if two souls quarrel and contend . . . differing and disputing, *both are wrong*" (italics in the original English).[67] Consultation is the chief tool Bahá'ís use to arrive at collective decisions. Many books, talks, videos, and courses have been prepared to refine the Bahá'í community's understanding of the consultation process. Many Bahá'ís who have become experts at consultation have become professionally involved in conflict resolution and arbitration.

10 Disciplining Members

Any religious community that maintains moral and ethical standards has the problem of members violating those standards. In the nineteenth century, many American Protestant churches punished members in a variety of ways, such as forcing them to stand before the congregation and confess their sin or denying them access to communion. Because people could easily change churches, that sanction ceased to be applied in many cases, though all denominations reserved the right to defrock a clergyman for flagrant violation of their standards.

Membership in the Bahá'í community comes with certain rights: the right to vote and be voted for; the right to contribute money to the Bahá'í funds, which only accept contributions from members; and the right to attend Feast, the monthly meeting of Bahá'í community members. Certain violations of Bahá'í law can result in loss of some or all of the rights of Bahá'í community membership. Bahá'ís without administrative rights nevertheless are considered Bahá'ís and can attend events that are open to the public. A Bahá'í has the right to withdraw from the Bahá'í community at

---

[67] 'Abdu'l-Bahá, *Tablets of the Divine Plan*, 53.

any time; the Bahá'í authoritative texts do not describe such an action as spiritually damaging (they do not describe the existence of a hell, for example). Former Bahá'ís should not experience a social stigma for withdrawal, either.

11 Persecution of the Bahá'í Community

As we have already noted, during the Bábí period (1844–53) the Bábí communities across Iran were often subject to Iranian army operations, and their defensive efforts were crushed, with considerable loss of life. One particular incident after the martyrdom of the Báb in 1850 is notable: a small group of Bábís in Tehran plotted to assassinate the Shah, in retaliation for his decision to have the Báb executed. The plot failed, and a pogrom against the Bábís in Tehran resulted in the deaths of hundreds of Bábís, including Ṭáhirih and other prominent leaders. It was the incident that caused Bahá'u'lláh's imprisonment in the Black Pit and his subsequent exile to Baghdad.

Once Bahá'u'lláh declared himself "He whom God shall make manifest" in 1863, he set out to reform and revitalize the Bábí community, which became the Bahá'í community over the next decade. The Bahá'í community grew much more quietly and did not resist persecution; Bahá'ís did not take defensive actions. Persecution continued but varied from city to city, depending on the attitudes of the local Shí'í clergy toward the Bahá'í community. In a few places there were even clergy who secretly converted to the Bahá'í Faith or were sympathetic. The Iranian army did not get involved. In cities with embassies or consulates, Bahá'ís often developed contacts with foreign officials, and, since the Iranian government would be embarrassed by violence against the Bahá'ís (which was reported in European and American newspapers), the government generally opposed efforts to persecute them. This was especially true in Tehran, the capital. Bahá'ís fleeing persecution in Yazd and Isfahan, where it was particularly severe, often settled in Tehran or crossed the border and settled in Ashkhabad, capital of Russian Turkmenistan.

Because of the steady flow of refugees coming to Tehran, that Bahá'í community developed capacities to assist them. One Isfahani Bahá'í who settled in Tehran opened a tile-making factory and hired his fellow Isfahani refugees, who all settled on one lane to assist each other. A prominent Tehran pharmacist who was a Bahá'í purchased a large house near his own that became, in effect, a resettlement center. An arriving Bahá'í family was settled in one room of the house until the husband could obtain work, sometimes through other Bahá'ís. The pharmacist's son was married to the daughter of the royal executioner, who became favorably disposed to the Bahá'í Faith and provided warnings whenever he was charged with the arrest of Bahá'ís.

The city's Bahá'í women reached out to the Muslim wives of Bahá'ís to teach the Faith to them (because of the social norms of the time, men were able to be exposed to a new Faith in public and convert, but women were much more restricted). If a Bahá'í was arrested in another city and sent to Tehran for trial or imprisonment, a Bahá'í woman would claim to be the man's sister and would visit him to make sure he had food and to find out how he was doing. Sometimes the Tehran Bahá'í women had to coordinate their efforts because so many men were in prison. Groups of women would go to government offices or even seek an audience with the Shah to make a petition regarding certain prisoners or to complain about treatment (and sometimes treatment of themselves, if they were abused when they insisted on seeing a prisoner). In some cases, they were the only ones who could remove the bodies of martyred Bahá'ís from the street.[68]

Because Tehran came to have such a large Bahá'í community and was itself a relatively safe city, it became the center of many important innovations. In 1877 a group of prominent Tehran Bahá'ís became aware of Bahá'u'lláh's call for the formation of consultative councils and decided to function as such a body for the city. They began to keep minutes and organized a Bahá'í fund; they even settled personal disputes between Bahá'ís. But Bahá'u'lláh asked them to disband in 1882, presumably because they were a self-appointed, ad hoc body.

Starting in 1887, Bahá'u'lláh appointed four individuals as Hands of the Cause of God – experienced Bahá'ís whom he could entrust with important missions. Because the Bahá'í community was still very much embedded in

[68] Moojan Momen, *The Bahá'í Communities of Iran, 1851–1921, vol. 1: The North of Iran*, 28, 31–4, 46, 48–9.

Islamic culture and was still used to deferring to authority, he had to choose men who would not assert a position over others or assume a clerical role. The four resided in Tehran, began to organize the Bahá'ís there, and traveled around the country to strengthen Bahá'í groups elsewhere. In 1897 'Abdu'l-Bahá asked them to organize a consultative body for Tehran, and possibly they asked a large group of prominent Bahá'í men to serve as electors to select members of the body, in addition to themselves. It may have been the first election in the Bahá'í world; the American Bahá'ís held their first elections in 1897 as well. The twelve members of the consultative assembly included the four Hands of the Cause, plus one Bahá'í of Jewish background and another of Zoroastrian background; the integration of the different ethnic groups into one Bahá'í community was underway. By 1913 the Hands were no longer serving on the body, and its entire membership was elected. The consultative council evolved into the "Central Spiritual Assembly," which functioned simultaneously to coordinate Bahá'í activities in Tehran and in all of Iran. From it, in 1934, came two separate spiritual assemblies, one local and one national in jurisdiction.[69]

With the development of consultative coordination, the Tehran community began to organize, in spite of persecution. In 1897 a Bahá'í opened a private school to educate Bahá'í boys; in 1898 Sunday school–type children's classes were started as well. In 1900 the community was able to open a formal private school for boys. A school for girls followed in 1911 with the help of the American Bahá'í women who had recently arrived. The Tarbiyat Schools for Boys and Girls evolved into what may have been the highest-quality private school in Iran, attracting many children of wealthy and powerful non-Bahá'ís, partly because the school did not include the Bahá'í Faith in its daily curriculum.[70]

In 1907, a Bahá'í started classes to train male Bahá'ís in religious subjects, so they could answer difficult questions; classes for women followed. In 1909 a group of Bahá'í physicians, including Dr. Susan Moody, a Chicago

---

[69] Moojan Momen, *The Bahá'í Communities of Iran, 1851–1921, vol. 1: The North of Iran*, 89, 92.

[70] Soli Shahvar, *The Forgotten Schools: The Baha'is and Modern Education in Iran, 1899–1934*, 96.

Baha'i, opened the Sihhat Hospital.[71] It served the public for free and was one of the few facilities that could provide medical assistance to women, since at that time male physicians could not examine female patients.

Because Bahá'ís were banned from public bathhouses (which were open to Muslims only), and as Bahá'u'lláh had forbidden the use of the stagnant rinsing pools of public baths (the water was changed only a few times a year), with Bahá'u'lláh commanding rinsing in clean running water instead, Bahá'í communities in many Iranian cities opened public bathhouses with showers, then an innovation in Iran and a great improvement for public health. Many Bahá'í-owned businesses established bathing facilities for their workers and families as well.[72]

In the second decade of the twentieth century, the Central Spiritual Assembly organized Shirkat-i-Nawnahálán (sometimes translated as "The Children's Company"). Parents bought bonds in the company, often in the names of their children, and the company invested the income in businesses, usually of Bahá'ís, since the courts could not be counted on to enforce debts owed by non-Bahá'ís to Bahá'ís. The result was in effect a private Bahá'í bank, overseen and guaranteed by the Central Spiritual Assembly, whose integrity was trusted by the Bahá'ís.

In a country lacking a stable banking system, reliable courts, a clear legal framework, unemployment compensation, insurance, and pension systems, the Shirkat-i-Nawnahálán gave the Bahá'í community financial stability and a safety net. Combined with the strong emphasis on education – illiteracy was eliminated among even the Iranian Bahá'í women by the mid twentieth century – and the generally improved health and longevity, the Bahá'í community gradually went from poverty to prosperity by the mid twentieth century. The guidance by Bahá'u'lláh and 'Abdu'l-Bahá channeled the Bahá'í response to persecution away from violence and to construction of a peaceful, prosperous community. It is the first and greatest example of what the Universal House of Justice has called *constructive resilience*: the effort to respond to persecution through positive action.

---

[71] Momen, *The Bahá'í Communities of Iran*, *vol. 1*, 97.

[72] Seena B. Fazel and Dominic Parviz Brookshaw, *The Bahá'ís of Iran: Socio-historical Studies*, 124–5, 128.

Bahá'ís in other countries have followed the same path. In mid-twentieth-century South Africa, Bahá'ís formed a multiracial and multiethnic community to the extent the apartheid laws would allow. Since governing boards of organizations could not be diverse in membership, the Bahá'ís elected only blacks to their Spiritual Assemblies, so that the principal minority ran the community. In contemporary Egypt, Bahá'ís have been imprisoned and have suffered from arson and discrimination.[73] They have engaged in a long legal battle in order to obtain the right to have the word "Bahá'í" added to their national identification cards, which only allowed the religious choices of Jew, Christian, or Muslim, none of which are acceptable to Bahá'ís. Without such a card, Egyptians cannot carry out many necessary day to day activities. Bahá'ís fearlessly appeared on Arab television to demand their rights in spite of the risk of imprisonment. They were ultimately allowed to put a dash in the religion field.

The situation of the Bahá'ís in other Islamic countries varies considerably. In nations dominated by Iran, their situation is serious; in Yemen currently, four Bahá'ís are in prison, and one has been sentenced to death for his religion. In other countries they may be tolerated but suffer some level of discrimination.

12 Bahá'í Teachings for Preventing Violence at a Societal and Global Level

Bahá'u'lláh's principles for a world civilization were subsequently elaborated upon by Shoghi Effendi and the Universal House of Justice. In 1936, the former summarized the Bahá'í vision of humanity's future this way:

> The unity of the human race, as envisaged by Bahá'u'lláh, implies the establishment of a world commonwealth in which all nations, races, creeds and classes are closely and permanently united, and in which the autonomy of its state members and the personal freedom and initiative of the

---

[73] "Egypt," in Paul Marshall and Nina Shea, *Silenced: How Apostasy and Blasphemy Codes are Choking Freedom Worldwide* (Oxford: Oxford University Press, 2011), 2.

individuals that compose them are definitely and completely safeguarded. This commonwealth must, as far as we can visualize it, consist of a world legislature, whose members will, as the trustees of the whole of mankind, ultimately control the entire resources of all the component nations, and will enact such laws as shall be required to regulate the life, satisfy the needs and adjust the relationships of all races and peoples. A world executive, backed by an international Force, will carry out the decisions arrived at, and apply the laws enacted by, this world legislature, and will safeguard the organic unity of the whole commonwealth. A world tribunal will adjudicate and deliver its compulsory and final verdict in all and any disputes that may arise between the various elements constituting this universal system.[74]

After summarizing the governing system of this world commonwealth, Shoghi Effendi turned to the common standards that will shape its society:

A mechanism of world inter-communication will be devised, embracing the whole planet, freed from national hindrances and restrictions, and functioning with marvellous swiftness and perfect regularity. A world metropolis will act as the nerve center of a world civilization, the focus towards which the unifying forces of life will converge and from which its energizing influences will radiate. A world language will either be invented or chosen from among the existing languages and will be taught in the schools of all the federated nations as an auxiliary to their mother tongue. A world script, a world literature, a uniform and universal system of currency, of weights and measures, will simplify and facilitate intercourse and understanding among the nations and races of mankind.[75]

[74] Shoghi Effendi Rabbani, *The World Order of Bahá'u'lláh*, 203.
[75] Shoghi Effendi Rabbani, *The World Order of Bahá'u'lláh*, 203.

Then Shoghi Effendi described some characteristics of global civilization:

> In such a world society, science and religion, the two most potent forces in human life, will be reconciled, will cooperate, and will harmoniously develop. The press will, under such a system, while giving full scope to the expression of the diversified views and convictions of mankind, cease to be mischievously manipulated by vested interests, whether private or public, and will be liberated from the influence of contending governments and peoples. The economic resources of the world will be organized, its sources of raw materials will be tapped and fully utilized, its markets will be coordinated and developed, and the distribution of its products will be equitably regulated.[76]

He offered a vision of the devotion of heretofore wasted resources to beneficial ends:

> National rivalries, hatreds, and intrigues will cease, and racial animosity and prejudice will be replaced by racial amity, understanding and cooperation. The causes of religious strife will be permanently removed, economic barriers and restrictions will be completely abolished, and the inordinate distinction between classes will be obliterated. Destitution on the one hand, and gross accumulation of ownership on the other, will disappear. The enormous energy dissipated and wasted on war, whether economic or political, will be consecrated to such ends as will extend the range of human inventions and technical development, to the increase of the productivity of mankind, to the extermination of disease, to the extension of scientific research, to the raising of the standard of physical health, to the sharpening and refinement of the human brain, to the

---

[76] Shoghi Effendi Rabbani, *The World Order of Bahá'u'lláh*, 203–4.

exploitation of the unused and unsuspected resources of
the planet, to the prolongation of human life, and to the
furtherance of any other agency that can stimulate the
intellectual, the moral, and spiritual life of the entire
human race.[77]

He closed his account of the world to come by linking its achievement to
acceptance of the revelation of Bahá'u'lláh:

> A world federal system, ruling the whole earth and exercis-
> ing unchallengeable authority over its unimaginably vast
> resources, blending and embodying the ideals of both the
> East and the West, liberated from the curse of war and its
> miseries, and bent on the exploitation of all the available
> sources of energy on the surface of the planet, a system in
> which Force is made the servant of Justice, whose life is
> sustained by its universal recognition of one God and by its
> allegiance to one common Revelation – such is the goal
> towards which humanity, impelled by the unifying forces of
> life, is moving.[78]

The future world being described is the Bahá'í equivalent of the millen-
nium, the Kingdom of God on Earth, even though the Bahá'í language is
very different from biblical descriptions such as "And I saw a new heaven
and a new earth: for the first heaven and the first earth were passed
away.... And I John saw the holy city, new Jerusalem, coming down
from God out of heaven, prepared as a bride adorned for her husband"
(Revelation 21:1–2). It is a world where structural violence has been
eliminated.

Shoghi Effendi noted that "unification of the whole of mankind is the
hall-mark of the stage which human society is now approaching. Unity of
family, of tribe, of city-state, and nation have been successively attempted

[77] Shoghi Effendi Rabbani, *The World Order of Bahá'u'lláh*, 204.
[78] Shoghi Effendi Rabbani, *The World Order of Bahá'u'lláh*, 204.

and fully established."[79] The Bahá'í authoritative texts say that a series of stages will be necessary before a world civilization is achieved and that the early stages will be achieved with little or no Bahá'í involvement.

Fifty years after Shoghi Effendi penned these passages, the Universal House of Justice issued a statement to the peoples of the world in 1986 titled *The Promise of World Peace*. It identified a "paralyzing contradiction" in human affairs:

> On the one hand, people of all nations proclaim not only their readiness but their longing for peace and harmony, for an end to the harrowing apprehensions tormenting their daily lives. On the other, uncritical assent is given to the proposition that human beings are incorrigibly selfish and aggressive and thus incapable of erecting a social system at once progressive and peaceful, dynamic and harmonious, a system giving free play to individual creativity and initiative but based on co-operation and reciprocity.[80]

The message noted that "peoples are ingenious enough to invent yet other forms of warfare, and to use food, raw materials, finance, industrial power, ideology, and terrorism to subvert one another in an endless quest for supremacy and dominion," so banning nuclear and biochemical weapons is not sufficient; a universal framework is needed instead. The message singled out a series of issues that such a framework needed to resolve, issues that were the cause of much of the structural violence in the world:[81]

> Racism ... perpetrates too outrageous a violation of the dignity of human beings to be countenanced under any pretext. Racism retards the unfoldment of the boundless

---

[79] Shoghi Effendi Rabbani, *The World Order of Bahá'u'lláh*, 202.

[80] Universal House of Justice, *The Promise of World Peace*, para. 7.

[81] Universal House of Justice, *The Promise of World Peace*, para. 25.

potentialities of its victims, corrupts its perpetrators, and blights human progress. . . .

The inordinate disparity between rich and poor, a source of acute suffering, keeps the world in a state of instability, virtually on the brink of war. Few societies have dealt effectively with this situation. The solution calls for the combined application of spiritual, moral and practical approaches. . . .

Unbridled nationalism, as distinguished from a sane and legitimate patriotism, must give way to a wider loyalty, to the love of humanity as a whole. Bahá'u'lláh's statement is: "The earth is but one country, and mankind its citizens." The concept of world citizenship is a direct result of the contraction of the world into a single neighbourhood through scientific advances and of the indisputable interdependence of nations. Love of all the world's peoples does not exclude love of one's country. The advantage of the part in a world society is best served by promoting the advantage of the whole. . . .

Religious strife, throughout history, has been the cause of innumerable wars and conflicts, a major blight to progress, and is increasingly abhorrent to the people of all faiths and no faith. . . . The challenge facing the religious leaders of mankind is . . . to ask themselves whether they cannot, in humility before their Almighty Creator, submerge their theological differences in a great spirit of mutual forbearance that will enable them to work together for the advancement of human understanding and peace.

The emancipation of women, the achievement of full equality between the sexes, is one of the most important, though less acknowledged prerequisites of peace. The denial of such equality perpetrates an injustice against one half of the world's population and promotes in men harmful attitudes and habits that are carried from the family to the workplace, to political life, and ultimately to international relations. . . .

> The cause of universal education, which has already
> enlisted in its service an army of dedicated people from
> every faith and nation, deserves the utmost support that
> the governments of the world can lend it. For ignorance is
> indisputably the principal reason for the decline and fall of
> peoples and the perpetuation of prejudice.[82]

Racism, the extremes of wealth and poverty, unbridled nationalism,
religious strife, the emancipation of women, and lack of education are all
matters first expounded on by Bahá'u'lláh, directly or directly, then elaborated on by 'Abdu'l-Bahá and Shoghi Effendi. As the civil rights movement
demonstrated, changing laws is not adequate for bringing about
a thoroughgoing change of culture and social organization in order to
eliminate structural violence. While rapidly mounting international problems may force humanity to institute many reforms at the legal and
governmental level, the necessary cultural changes to bring about a world
without these forms of injustice will require centuries. Ideally, they need to
be replaced by the values and principles of religion, which makes their
elimination a matter of faith and of personal spiritual struggle. This is the
approach the Bahá'ís are taking.

13 Growth and Development of the International Bahá'í Community, 1892–Present

As already noted, at the time of Bahá'u'lláh's passing in 1892 the Bahá'í
Faith had spread from Iran to much of the Middle East, South Asia, and
Central Asia, in every case primarily to Shi'i and Sunni Muslims, though
Iranian Jews and Zoroastrians, Lebanese and Egyptian Christians, and
possibly Burmese Buddhists had also joined. The Bahá'í community had
grown to perhaps 100,000, 98 percent of whom lived in Iran. 'Abdu'l-Bahá
oversaw an expansion of the Bahá'í Faith to the United States and Canada,
where about 1,500 converts resided by his passing in 1921; to England,
France, and Germany, where the communities numbered less than 100 each;

---

[82] Universal House of Justice, *The Promise of World Peace*, paras. 29–34.

and to Hawaii, Australia, Japan, and China, where handfuls of Bahá'ís could be found.

During Shoghi Effendi's ministry (1921–63), the initial focus was on establishing local and National Spiritual Assemblies, an effort that took about fifteen years. At that point (the mid-1930s), political conditions deteriorated in many countries. The Iranian government closed all Bahá'í schools in 1934 and banned Bahá'í publishing. The Bahá'í Faith was banned in Iraq and Bahá'í properties were confiscated, including Bahá'u'lláh's house in Baghdad, which was a site of pilgrimage. Stalin destroyed the Bahá'í communities in the Soviet Union, confiscated the Bahá'í House of Worship in Ashkhabat, banned all Bahá'í organization, and exiled many Bahá'ís to Siberia. The Nazis banned the Bahá'í Faith in Germany and Austria. The French Bahá'ís dispersed during the occupation.

While the Faith had grown in India, Burma, Australia, and New Zealand, the communities were still small and immature. The North American believers were the only ones who had developed mature institutions and had the numbers and the freedom to spread the Faith worldwide, so Shoghi Effendi gave them a Seven-Year Plan (1937–44). It called for the establishment of at least one local Spiritual Assembly in every American state and every Canadian province and the settling of at least one Bahá'í in every republic in Latin America. As World War II spread across the world, Latin America was one of the few areas with relative peace and stability. All the goals were achieved; the Bahá'í Faith was now established in every American state and every Canadian province. The efforts were so successful in Latin America that local Spiritual Assemblies (which require at least nine Bahá'ís residing in the same locality) were elected in ten countries. Women played a crucial role as pioneers (persons who settle in a new place and find a job in order to establish a Bahá'í community there) or as traveling Bahá'í teachers.

To make clear the spiritual values behind the first Seven-Year Plan (and, in general, behind spreading the Bahá'í Faith by teaching it to others), Shoghi Effendi penned an important epistle to the North American Bahá'ís, published as *The Advent of Divine Justice* in 1938. He emphasized that, as important as fashioning "outward instruments" and "administrative agencies" was, as well as initiating campaigns and raising funds, "the imponderable, the spiritual, factors, which are bound up with their own individual and inner lives, and with which are associated their human and social relationships, are no less urgent and vital, and demand constant scrutiny, continual self-examination, and heart-searching on their part, lest their value be impaired or their vital necessity be obscured and forgotten."[83] He expatiated at length on three spiritual prerequisites for success. The first was a

> rectitude of conduct, with its implications of justice, equity, truthfulness, honesty, fair-mindedness, reliability, and trustworthiness. . . . It must be constantly reflected in the business dealings of all its members, in their domestic lives, in all manner of employment, and in any service they may, in the future, render their government or people. . . . It must be demonstrated in the impartiality of every defender of the Faith against its enemies, in his fair-mindedness in recognizing any merits that enemy may possess, and in his honesty in discharging any obligations he may have towards him. It must constitute the brightest ornament of the life, the pursuits, the exertions, and the utterances of every Bahá'í teacher, whether laboring at home or abroad, whether in the front ranks of the teaching force, or occupying a less active and responsible position.[84]

The second spiritual prerequisite was a chaste and holy life, "with its implications of modesty, purity, temperance, decency, and clean-mindedness." It "involves no less than the exercise of moderation in all that pertains to dress, language, amusements, and all artistic and literary avocations."[85] Shoghi Effendi noted that it included abstinence from alcoholic beverages, a Bahá'í law the American believers had been aware of

[83] Shoghi Effendi Rabbani, *The Advent of Divine Justice*, 22.
[84] Shoghi Effendi Rabbani, *The Advent of Divine Justice*, 26.
[85] Shoghi Effendi Rabbani, *The Advent of Divine Justice*, 29.

since the first decade of the twentieth century but which had not been binding on them heretofore. He added that

> it must be remembered, however, that the maintenance of such a high standard of moral conduct is not to be associated or confused with any form of asceticism, or of excessive and bigoted puritanism. The standard inculcated by Bahá'u'lláh seeks, under no circumstances, to deny anyone the legitimate right and privilege to derive the fullest advantage and benefit from the manifold joys, beauties, and pleasures with which the world has been so plentifully enriched by an All-Loving Creator.[86]

The third spiritual prerequisite was "complete freedom from prejudice in their dealings with peoples of a different race, class, creed, or color." He elaborated on the subject at length:

> As to racial prejudice, the corrosion of which, for well-nigh a century, has bitten into the fiber, and attacked the whole social structure of American society, it should be regarded as constituting the most vital and challenging issue confronting the Bahá'í community at the present stage of its evolution. The ceaseless exertions which this issue of paramount importance calls for, the sacrifices it must impose, the care and vigilance it demands, the moral courage and fortitude it requires, the tact and sympathy it necessitates, invest this problem, which the American believers are still far from having satisfactorily resolved, with an urgency and importance that cannot be overestimated. White and Negro, high and low, young and old, whether newly converted to the Faith or not, all who stand identified with it must participate in, and lend their assistance, each according to his or her capacity, experience, and opportunities, to the common task

[86] Shoghi Effendi Rabbani, *The Advent of Divine Justice*, 33.

of fulfilling the instructions, realizing the hopes, and following the example, of ʿAbdu'l-Bahá. Whether colored or noncolored, neither race has the right, or can conscientiously claim, to be regarded as absolved from such an obligation, as having realized such hopes, or having faithfully followed such an example. A long and thorny road, beset with pitfalls, still remains untraveled, both by the white and the Negro exponents of the redeeming Faith of Bahá'u'lláh. On the distance they cover, and the manner in which they travel that road, must depend, to an extent which few among them can imagine, the operation of those intangible influences which are indispensable to the spiritual triumph of the American believers and the material success of their newly launched enterprise.[87]

Shoghi Effendi illustrated each of the three with several pages of quotations from Bahá'u'lláh and ʿAbdu'l-Bahá. In this way, he elaborated on Bahá'u'lláh's ethical and spiritual admonitions to the "true seeker" and applied them to the needs and concerns of the mid-twentieth century American Bahá'ís and their efforts to spread the Faith.

After a two-year hiatus, Shoghi Effendi gave the North American Bahá'ís a second Seven-Year Plan (1946–53). It aimed to reestablish the Bahá'í communities in Germany and Japan, to establish new Bahá'í communities in a dozen other European countries, and to elect one National Spiritual Assembly for all of South America, one for all of Central America, and one for Canada. The Bahá'í Temple outside Chicago was to be completed. Again, all the goals were achieved. The Bahá'í Faith was now solidly but thinly established all across the western hemisphere and Western Europe. The creation of the Iron Curtain, however, cut off the scattered Bahá'ís in Eastern Europe and the Soviet Union.

Shoghi Effendi immediately followed the plan with a Ten-Year Crusade (1953–63). The choice of the word "crusade" reflected the Persian title of the plan – Jihád-i-Kabir-i-Akbar or "the Greatest of the Great Jiháds" – and

---

[87] Shoghi Effendi Rabbani, *The Advent of Divine Justice*, 22, 33.

emphasized both its importance and the immense scale of the non-violent effort. All twelve of the National Spiritual Assemblies that then existed received goals. Almost every country in Africa, most major island groups in the Caribbean and Pacific, and the remaining non-Communist countries in Asia were to form numerous local Bahá'í communities, with the goal of electing forty-five new National Spiritual Assemblies, raising the total to fifty-seven. Thousands of Bahá'ís moved to new countries or cities, found themselves housing and jobs, and began to tell neighbors and work colleagues about their religion. Every country but one – Afghanistan – elected its National Spiritual Assembly by April 1962.

Shoghi Effendi also encouraged the spread of the Bahá'í Faith beyond the urban upper and middle classes to the rural masses. As a result, 5,000 people became Bahá'ís in the remote Mentawai Islands of Indonesia; 40,000 Ugandans, Congolese, and Kenyans converted; Quechua and Aymara villagers began to join the Faith in Bolivia; and Bahá'í communities began to develop on the coral atolls of the Gilbert Islands (now called Kiribati). In 1963, when the Universal House of Justice was first elected, the Bahá'í Faith had grown to over 400,000 members.[88] Even in that year, two-thirds to three-quarters of the world's Bahá'ís were Iranian and resided in that country.

With growth came persecution in Egypt, Morocco, Indonesia, and, to a minor extent, the British-controlled Pacific and a few sub-Saharan African countries. The Faith remained illegal in all Communist countries except Cuba. A major attempt to destroy the Bahá'í Faith in Iran in 1955 resulted in violence against Bahá'ís, martyrdoms, destruction of houses and businesses, unrelenting attacks on the radio and in newspapers, and the temporary confiscation and destruction of several important community properties. An unprecedented media response by the Bahá'ís outside Iran generated public and diplomatic pressure, forcing the end of the overt persecution. Because a Bahá'í temple could not be built in Iran, three were built elsewhere: in Uganda, Australia, and Germany.

---

[88] This is a summary of information in Stockman, *The Bahá'í Faith: A Guide for the Perplexed*, 150–3.

The mid-1960s through the early 1970s was a period of social ferment in much of the world. The Bahá'í Faith saw very rapid growth in membership as a tiny fraction of the disillusioned sought refuge in the Bahá'í vision of a unified and diverse world. The techniques that took the Bahá'í Faith to the rural masses were utilized in more and more countries, including the United States, where some 15,000 rural African Americans in South Carolina became Bahá'ís in the early 1970s. The Faith spread on American Indian reservations and to migrant farm workers as well. Many college students joined. The number of American Bahá'ís, which stood at 5,000 in 1945 and 10,000 in 1963, grew to 15,000 by 1967 and 60,000 by 1973. Subsequently the number grew to 100,000 in 1986, 150,000 in 2003, and 177,000 in 2019.[89] Worldwide, the numbers reached 3 million by the 1980s and 5 million by the twenty-first century. The Iranian Bahá'í community, which remained at about 300,000, became a small fraction of the total membership; India, with 1 to 2 million Bahá'ís, became the largest community; several other nations in Africa and South America had more than 100,000 members.[90] The number of National Spiritual Assemblies reached 170. The number of local Spiritual Assemblies worldwide peaked at over 17,000 and dropped to 12,000 when efforts to maintain them in rural areas were scaled back and when official government civil boundaries were adopted (resulting in one Spiritual Assembly per township rather than one per village or hamlet). Additional temples were completed in Panama, Samoa, India, and Chile, establishing one on every continent.

The very rapid spread of the Bahá'í Faith, especially in rural areas where the literacy level was low, transportation was poor, and the population was unused to electing their own religious leadership, created serious problems for consolidating the gains. Some rural Bahá'ís moved to the burgeoning cities and disappeared. Many local Spiritual Assemblies were inactive and unable to hold Feasts (the monthly Bahá'í community meeting) or plan their

---

[89] Robert Stockman, "United States Bahá'í Membership and Enrollment Statistics, 1894–2017," author's personal papers.

[90] Most of this essay focuses on the Bahá'í experience in Iran and the United States for two reasons: until 1963, they were the two largest and most important communities; and far more scholarship is available about them than about any other national Bahá'í communities.

own annual reelection. The mass teaching effort was not a failure: some rural Bahá'ís became very active and taught the Faith to their children, resulting in stable, multigenerational Bahá'í communities of indigenous peoples. Bahá'í radio stations in rural areas helped establish Bahá'í values and prayers widely, even among people who were not registered as members. Low literacy materials and translations of Bahá'í literature into 800 languages helped as well. But the growth in the developing countries underscored the problem of spiritually transforming believers to become active in the Faith and involved in solving the problems of their societies in a nonpartisan fashion.

In 1996, the Universal House of Justice initiated a twenty-five year effort (1996–2021) to develop a system whereby people could be brought into the Bahá'í community systematically and consolidated effectively. As the effort progressed, new elements were introduced. The principle behind the entire process was simple: that the Bahá'í Faith needed to develop the ability to empower everyone, producing a community that is not dependent on a few highly active members. The concern was to avoid what was often referred to as the "congregational mindset" where a congregation was dependent on a clergyman and a few paid staff to maintain their religious life. The nature of the empowerment was also important: to teach the Bahá'í Faith to others, exemplify it in one's own life and in the Bahá'í community, and improve society through achievable projects for social and economic development. Behind the entire effort lay the understanding that the structural violence inherent in most societies around the world could be best combated through the individual transformation and constructive activism of everyone, not just the Bahá'ís. As the Universal House of Justice explained in 2013, "capacity building is the watchword of these plans: they aim at enabling the protagonists of collective effort to strengthen the spiritual foundations of villages and neighborhoods, to address certain of their social and economic needs, and to contribute to the discourses prevalent in society."[91] By 2015, the effort came to possess the following elements.

[91] Universal House of Justice to the Bahá'ís of Iran, March 2, 2013, 4; https://universalhouseofjustice.bahai.org/involvement-life-society/20130302_001 (accessed July 23, 2019).

13.1 Study Circles

Starting in 1996, the Universal House of Justice called for the creation of systematic curricula that would provide Bahá'ís, consulting together in study circles, with a solid understanding of the Bahá'í teachings and training on how to implement them. Various programs were initiated or refined around the world. In Colombia, where the number of Bahá'ís went from a few hundred to 30,000 in the early 1970s, the urgent need to consolidate the growth led to the development of the Ruhi curriculum, which was already at an advanced state of development in 1996. Over the next decade it spread until, in 2005, the Universal House of Justice declared it the universal curriculum to be used until at least 2021.

The Ruhi books provided knowledge and fostered memorization of passages from Bahá'í sacred texts, but they were not a catechism: their main focus was imparting skills to set people on a path of service to others. Book 1 taught people to conduct devotional programs in their houses (which consist of reciting or singing selections of prayers and scriptures) and emphasized use of the arts and the composition of music, thereby empowering people to organize their own worship. Book 2 focused on visiting people in their homes to discuss spiritual subjects. Book 3 provided materials and advice for conducting classes focused on virtues for children. Book 4 discussed the lives of the Báb and Bahá'u'lláh and ways to tell stories about them. Book 5 contained materials to teach classes for older children. Book 6 covered teaching the Bahá'í Faith to others. Book 7 provided training to be a Ruhi tutor.

The Ruhi books were fairly simple and generic, were easy to translate into many languages, and did not require special art materials or extra written materials. They were designed so that groups could go through them together with the assistance of a tutor who did not need extensive training. They were, however, lengthy: on average, each required about forty hours to complete.[92] Subsequently, three more books were added, about the Bahá'í Covenant, progressive revelation, and accompanying others in service. More are planned. They have been translated into scores of languages, including Nepalese, Mongolian, Quechua, and Swahili.

---

[92] Stockman, *The Bahá'í Faith: A Guide for the Perplexed*, 193.

13.2 Core Activities

The spread of the Ruhi curriculum and the tasks for which the books trained people set the stage for designating a series of core activities for the Bahá'í community to pursue. In April 2002 the Universal House of Justice designated three core activities: study circles (where the Ruhi books are studied); children's classes (to teach virtues and Bahá'í principles); and devotional programs (informal gatherings for worship). These were not meant to replace the other activities Bahá'í communities already had: the Nineteen-Day Feast, firesides (informal gatherings to discuss the Bahá'í teachings with inquirers), and deepenings (gatherings to study a Bahá'í text or teaching in detail). In practice, however, there were only so many human resources available, so that many deepenings were replaced by study circles and many firesides were replaced by devotionals. Most Bahá'í communities already had classes for their own children, but the new emphasis was on children in general, with the classes focused on virtues rather than on Bahá'í history and teachings.

Later the Universal House of Justice added a fourth core activity, empowerment meetings for junior youth (aged eleven to fourteen years), who are at a crucial age to learn personal empowerment and the importance of service to others. Youth (those fifteen and older) mentored the junior youth. To foster the effort, Ruhi Book 5 was replaced by three books that provided junior youth training and activities. By 2010, junior youth programs had become the central Bahá'í outreach effort in many places.

13.3 Social Action and Public Discourse

The core activities were originally designed to consolidate new Bahá'ís and empower them to become active, but it was soon noted that, if non-Bahá'í children were being invited to classes, the parents could be invited to a study circle and often enjoyed it. But teaching the Bahá'í Faith to others was not the only concern of the Bahá'í community; Bahá'í principles had to be put into action through service and had to become the focus of dialogue with others about ways to solve local problems and ultimately reduce the structural violence many people faced, especially minorities and the poor.

Consequently, in 2010 the Universal House of Justice put the core activities in a larger context. First, it recommended that Bahá'ís focus their efforts on a neighborhood or village, so that they have a measurable impact locally. Second, it recommended the gradual introduction of social action: cleaning parks, tutoring children, planting trees, and other simple, basic activities that a small group of people could do together effectively. Third, social action was to be coupled with public discourse, discussion with people in the village or neighborhood about their needs and about ways everyone could get involved to address local problems through volunteerism and individual empowerment.

In practice, social action proved to be quite limited until there were many dozens of people involved in core activities; indeed, junior youth groups and children's classes often became the main social action efforts, with the children or youth doing service projects. Many children's class teachers were not Bahá'ís, and no pressure was put on them to convert. Public discourse also became an important Bahá'í activity, with such ongoing efforts as involvement in interfaith organizations finding a place in the overall framework of Bahá'í effort.

13.4 Organization

Core activities, social action, and public discourse required new developments in Bahá'í organization. National Spiritual Assemblies were responsible for huge areas and often could not support all local efforts adequately; on the other hand, since Bahá'í local Spiritual Assemblies were elected any place with nine or more Bahá'ís in a civil jurisdiction, there were a large number of Bahá'í communities with a very small number of members and many Bahá'ís living in civil jurisdictions with groups of fewer than nine Bahá'ís. To close the gap, as early as the 1980s the Universal House of Justice allowed the National Spiritual Assembly of the Bahá'ís of India to oversee the election of Regional Councils. In May 1997 the House formally announced the inauguration of Regional Councils, to be elected by all the members of the local Spiritual Assemblies in the region, generally by postal ballot. The United Kingdom eventually had four, for England, Scotland, Wales, and Northern Ireland. The United States elected four in 1997 and gradually split them; by 2017, it had twelve councils.

In 2002, the Universal House of Justice also directed National Spiritual Assemblies to divide their countries into manageable geographic units called *clusters*. The United States was divided into about 900 of them, typically consisting of a metropolitan area or a group of counties. In many cases, this brought about the coordination of several local Spiritual Assemblies, thereby pooling the resources of several communities. It also allowed Bahá'ís living outside the jurisdiction of Spiritual Assemblies to become involved. Regional Councils were given the responsibility to appoint committees or coordinators to encourage study circles, children's classes, junior youth groups, and other activities. Clusters were encouraged to make plans on a quarterly cycle, with a reflection meeting at the end of each quarter to consult about what was accomplished and to set goals for the next quarter. Only Bahá'ís can be elected to Spiritual Assemblies and attend Feast, but cluster activities, committees, and reflection meetings are open to anyone, regardless of their religion or lack thereof. In this way, Bahá'í communities sought to build a social movement capable of bringing about significant social change.

14 Constructive Resilience in Iran

Iran's Islamic Revolution in 1978–79 changed the legal and social status of all religious and ethnic minorities in Iran. But while the Iranian Constitution recognized Christianity, Judaism, and Zoroastrianism and gave their members certain civil rights (which were not always respected), the Bahá'í Faith was not recognized at all: its institutions were banned, and the legal rights of its members were entirely denied. Since 1978, the Bahá'ís in Iran – some 300,000 strong – have not had the freedom to practice their faith openly. Some 200 Bahá'ís have been executed for their faith, thousands have been imprisoned, and tens of thousands have fled the country. Bahá'í holy places have been confiscated and often razed to the ground. Bahá'í cemeteries have been confiscated and desecrated. An entirely Bahá'í village was bulldozed. Bahá'ís are discriminated against in courts, making it difficult to collect insurance payments, obtain inheritances, or seek redress for crimes committed against them. Bahá'ís of university age have been systematically denied admission to Iran's universities, and if they are admitted they are often told – right before a semester ends or they are about to get their degree – that they must deny their Faith to be allowed to complete their studies.

The Bahá'ís' response to the gross violation of their rights as individuals and what has been termed an attempt at the genocide of a religious community has been constructive resilience, whereby Bahá'ís respond to persecution through acts of service. As previously noted, this was the Bahá'í response to persecution from the beginning. In the early twentieth century, the Tehran Bahá'ís built remarkable community institutions, including high-quality schools open to all, a hospital that served anyone, and a savings and loan company.

By 1979, persecution had destroyed all those institutions, forcing the Bahá'ís to channel their efforts in other directions. Bahá'ís have been arrested and imprisoned for offering virtues classes to children and for providing tutoring on school subjects; in the 1980s, during the height of persecution, some were even executed for teaching such classes. By far the largest and most systematic Bahá'í response to persecution, however, has been the establishment of the Bahá'í Institute for Higher Education (BIHE), a grassroots private university to provide Iranian Bahá'í youth the education the government has systematically banned them from.

Repeated attempts to break up classes, confiscate equipment, harass Bahá'ís assisting, and arrest teachers and administrators have driven much of BIHE's work online. The students are in Iran, but the bulk of the instructors and administrators are not. Many courses are offered in English, so the English language is taught as well. The students do not pay, and most of the faculty serve for free. The resulting institution offers a bachelor's degree with over a dozen majors to an enrollment of about a thousand at any particular time. Some 100 graduates have come to North America or Europe for graduate study, and their BIHE Bachelors has been accepted, in spite of the fact that the institution, by definition, cannot be accredited or legally recognized in Iran. Many of the majors that are taught face-to-face focus on practical skills, such as dental hygiene or counseling. The BIHE has, as its overall purpose, to serve the people of Iran. One would be hard pressed to find another religious community in history that responded to executions, torture, confiscation, and discrimination by opening a university.

15 Constructive Engagement

The Universal House of Justice's overall goal in 1996 was to dedicate the upcoming twenty-five-year period to creating a framework that would lead to "entry by troops" – in other words, a rapid growth in the size of the international Bahá'í community. As that framework developed, the effort led away from systematic presentation of the Bahá'í teachings to masses of people and to an approach that demonstrates the teachings through social action instead, on the understanding that the resulting example would both attract people and bring about changes in culture. Some would join the Bahá'í community eventually; others would adopt some Bahá'í values and approaches to social change. The emphasis came to resemble the constructive resilience of the Iranian Bahá'í community.

No single term has yet been standardized to describe this process. Some extend the term "constructive resilience" to refer to this engagement in society by emphasizing the problem of structural violence on the people being served. Others have preferred to refer to "constructive engagement" to highlight the Bahá'í Faith's overall focus on building unity, whether through dialogue or action. Constructive engagement is an extension of the principles of constructive resilience, and the two lie on a spectrum of constructive activity.

Constructive engagement appears to be developing into the Bahá'í community's principal mode of involvement in society. In the past, proclamation of basic Bahá'í social principles – the equality of all people, the equality of men and women, the harmony of science and religion, spiritual solutions to economic problems, universal education, the oneness of religion, the need for a world government – were sufficient to attract people to the fold and influence social thought. But the world caught up to most of these principles, which no longer look as revolutionary as they did when ʿAbdu'l-Bahá proclaimed them in his talks to Western audiences in 1911–13. Furthermore, the Bahá'í community is now larger and understands the teachings in its authoritative texts more deeply. Thus it is in the position to actualize the teachings in order to create wider and wider circles of cooperation and concord.

In another sense, constructive engagement is the Bahá'í answer to non-violent civil disobedience as a mechanism for social change. In addition to the mandate that Bahá'ís remain non-violent, their scriptures call on them to be obedient to their government unless it demands that they renounce their faith in whole or in part. Consequently, Bahá'ís cannot be involved in efforts to change society that break the law; such actions would undermine legitimate authority, which is an essential ingredient in a unified and just society. From a Bahá'í point of view, even non-violent civil disobedience ultimately has structural violence built into it, because it uses strife and disunity to bring about change and undermines the basic structures of society. The purpose of constructive engagement goes beyond efforts to change laws and policies and seeks to change hearts and the culture itself.

16 Conclusion

The Bahá'í approach to violence begins with the creation of a community of believers striving to strengthen their relationship to God, to seek to investigate reality independently, to follow Bahá'u'lláh's ethical principles and laws ever more faithfully, and to actively apply them to their lives and communities. The principles delineate a world view based on the oneness of humanity and the unity, equality, and justice it implies. Unity is a complex ethical principle that begins with simple cooperation but aims for a unity of souls. It rejects partisanship and emphasizes a values-based system of communication called consultation. The concept of unity, however, does not assume that everyone will always cooperate voluntarily and in a reasonable fashion. Bahá'í governing bodies can make decisions by majority vote if unanimity is not possible. Within the Bahá'í community, sanctions – non-violent ones, but sanctions nevertheless – exist. Bahá'ís and their institutions are not allowed to use violence to protect themselves against persecution, which is rampant and severe in some parts of the world. In the international arena, the Bahá'í authoritative texts recognize the need to oppose an unjust invasion of a country by means of warfare, and thus the Bahá'í Faith has a theory of just war.

The Bahá'í community seeks through its core activities and its public discourse to move the world toward conditions where structural violence has been eliminated, where all have access to education, justice, and opportunity, where discrimination is ended, where crime is greatly reduced, and where relations among nations are regularized to the extent that warfare is abolished. The Bahá'í scriptures maintain that such a near-utopian order is only possible through a divinely revealed system of values voluntarily accepted and adhered to as a matter of trust and faith, for ethical systems and social theories created by philosophers have neither the universal appeal nor the depth of commitment that a religious value system can have. For over a century and a half, the Bahá'ís have been building an international community that strives to represent and reflect unity in diversity and to offer a vision of a new world civilization that goes far beyond non-violence and embodies deeper and broader efforts to achieve the unity of humankind.

Bibliography

ʿAbdu'l-Bahá Abbás. *Promulgation of Universal Peace*. Compiled by Howard MacNutt. 2nd ed. Wilmette, IL: Bahá'í Publishing Trust, 1982.

ʿAbdu'l-Bahá Abbás. *Some Answered Questions*. Newly revised translation by a committee at the Bahá'í World Centre. Haifa: Bahá'í World Centre, 2014.

ʿAbdu'l-Bahá Abbás. *Tablets of the Divine Plan*. Translated by Shoghi Effendi Rabbani. Rev. ed. 1977. Wilmette, IL: Bahá'í Publishing Trust, 1977.

Báb, The. *Selections from the Writings of the Báb*. Translated by Habib Taherzadeh. Haifa: Bahá'í World Centre, 1976.

Bahá'u'lláh, the Báb, and ʿAbdu'l-Bahá. *Bahá'í Prayers: A Selection of Prayers Revealed by Bahá'u'lláh, the Báb, and ʿAbdu'l-Bahá*. Wilmette, IL: Bahá'í Publishing Trust, 1991.

Bahá'u'lláh and ʿAbdu'l-Bahá. *Bahá'í World Faith: Selected Writings of Bahá'u'lláh and ʿAbdu'l-Bahá*. Wilmette, IL: Bahá'í Publishing Trust, 1971.

Bahá'u'lláh. *Days of Remembrance: Selections from the Writings of Bahá'u'lláh for the Bahá'í Holy Days*. Haifa: Bahá'í World Centre, 2016.

Bahá'u'lláh. Epistle to the Son of the Wolf. Translated by Shoghi Effendi Rabbani. Rev. ed. Wilmette, IL: Bahá'í Publishing Trust, 1976.

Bahá'u'lláh. *Gleanings from the Writings of Bahá'u'lláh*. Translated by Shoghi Effendi Rabbani. 2nd ed. Wilmette, IL: Bahá'í Publishing Trust, 1976.

Bahá'u'lláh. The Hidden Words. Translated by Shoghi Effendi. Wilmette, Ill.: Bahá'í Publishing Trust, 2003.

Bahá'u'lláh. The Kitáb-i-Aqdas: The Most Holy Book. Haifa: Bahá'í World Centre, 1992.

Bahá'u'lláh. The Seven Valleys and the Four Valleys. Translated by Marzieh Gail. Wilmette, IL: Bahá'í Publishing Trust, 1991.

Bahá'u'lláh. *The Summons of the Lord of Hosts: Tablets of Bahá'u'lláh*. Haifa: Bahá'í World Centre, 2002.

Bahá'u'lláh. *The Tabernacle of Unity: Bahá'u'lláh's Responses to Mánikchí Sáhib and Other Writings*. Haifa: Bahá'í World Centre, 2006.

Bahá'u'lláh. *Tablets of Bahá'u'lláh Revealed After the Kitáb-i-Aqdas*. Comp. Research Department of the Universal House of Justice. Translated by Habib Taherzadeh. Haifa: Bahá'í World Centre, 1978.

Balyuzi, H. M. *Bahá'u'lláh: The King of Glory*. Oxford: George Ronald, 1980.

Danesh, Hossain B. *The Violence-Free Society: A Gift for Our Children*. Ottawa, ON: The Canadian Association for Studies on the Bahá'í Faith, 1979. https://bahai-studies.ca/wp-content/uploads/2018/04/Violence-Free-Society.pdf (accessed July 13, 2019).

Fazel, Seena B., and Dominic Parviz Brookshaw. *The Bahá'ís of Iran: Socio-historical Studies*. London: Routledge, 2008.

Hornby, Helen, comp. and ed. *Lights of Guidance: A Bahá'í Reference File*. 2nd ed. New Delhi: Bahá'í Publishing Trust, 1988.

Hornby, Helen, comp. and ed. *Lights of Guidance: A Bahá'í Reference File*. 3rd ed. New Delhi: Bahá'í Publishing Trust, 1994.

Lawson, Todd. "The Baha'i Tradition: The Return of Joseph and the Peaceable Imagination." In John Renard, ed., *Fighting Words: Religion, Violence, and the Interpretation of Sacred Texts*. Berkeley: University of California Press, 2012, 135–57.

Lewis, Elizabeth. "What is Structural Violence?" www.thoughtco.com/structural-violence-4174956 (accessed July 13, 2019).

Marshall, Paul, and Nina Shea. *Silenced: How Apostasy and Blasphemy Codes are Choking Freedom Worldwide* (Oxford: Oxford University Press, 2011).

Momen, Moojan. *The Bahá'í Communities of Iran, 1851–1921, vol. 1: The North of Iran*. Oxford: George Ronald, 2015.

Momen, Moojan. "Messianic Concealment and Theophanic Disclosure." *Bahá'í Studies Review* 20 (2014): 51–67.

Momen, Moojan. "Mysticism and the Bahá'í Community." www
.momen.org/bahai2/mysticismbc.htm (accessed July 21, 2019).

Morrison, Gayle. *To Move the World*. Wilmette, IL: Bahá'í Publishing
Trust, 1982.

Rabbani, Shoghi Effendi. *The Advent of Divine Justice*. 3rd ed. Wilmette, IL:
Bahá'í Publishing Trust, 1971.

Rabbani, Shoghi Effendi. *Bahá'í Administration*. Wilmette, IL: Bahá'í
Publishing Trust, 1968.

Rabbani, Shoghi Effendi. *The Lights of Divine Guidance*, vol. 2. In *Ocean*
(electronic scripture library).

Rabbani, Shoghi Effendi. *The World Order of Bahá'u'lláh*. Wilmette, IL:
Bahá'í Publishing Trust, 1991.

Research Department of the Universal House of Justice, comp.
*Consultation: A Compilation: Extracts from the Writings and Utterances of
Bahá'u'lláh, 'Abdu'l-Bahá, Shoghi Effendi, and The Universal House of
Justice*. Wilmette, IL: Bahá'í Publishing Trust, 1980.

Research Department of the Universal House of Justice, comp. *Women:
Extracts from the Writings of Bahá'u'lláh, 'Abdu'l-Bahá, Shoghi Effendi
and the Universal House of Justice*. Thornhill, ON: Bahá'í Canada
Publications, 1986.

Saiei, Nader. "From Oppression to Empowerment." *Journal of Bahá'í
Studies* 26.1–2 (2016): 27–53.

Saiedi, Nader. *Gate of the Heart*. Waterloo, ON: Wilfrid Laurier University
Press, 2008.

Saiedi, Nader. *Logos and Civilization*. Bethesda: University Press of
Maryland, 2000.

Shahvar, Soli. *The Forgotten Schools: The Baha'is and Modern Education in
Iran, 1899–1934*. London: Tauris Academic Studies, 2009.

Stockman, Robert. *'Abdu'l-Bahá in America*. Wilmette, IL: Bahá'í Publishing
Trust, 2012.

Stockman, Robert. "United States Bahá'í Membership and Enrollment Statistics, 1894–2017." Author's personal papers.

Stockman, Robert. *The Bahá'í Faith in America, vol. 1: Origins, 1892–1900.* Wilmette, IL. Bahá'í Publishing Trust, 1985.

Stockman, Robert. *The Bahá'í Faith in America, vol. 2: Early Expansion, 1900–1912.* Oxford: George Ronald, 1995.

Stockman, Robert. *The Bahá'í Faith: A Guide for the Perplexed.* London: Bloomsbury, 2013.

Universal House of Justice, The. *A Compilation of Compilations, Vol. I.* Maryborough, Victoria, Australia: Bahá'í Publications Australia, 1991.

Universal House of Justice, The. *The Promise of World Peace.* In *Ocean* (electronic scripture library).

Universal House of Justice to the Bahá'ís of Iran. March 2, 2013. https://universalhouseofjustice.bahai.org/involvement-life-society/20130302_001 (accessed July 23, 2019).

Zarandí, Muḥammad Nabíl-i-ʿAʾzam. *The Dawn-Breakers: Nabíl's Narrative of the Early Days of the Bahá'í Revelation.* New York: Bahá'í Publishing Committee, 1932.

Zarqání, Mírzá Maḥmúd. *Maḥmúd's Diary: The Diary of Mírzá Maḥmúd-i-Zarqání Chronicling ʿAbdu'l-Bahá's Journey to America.* Oxford: George Ronald, 1998.

Cambridge Elements ≡

Religion and Violence

James R. Lewis
University of Tromsø

James R. Lewis is Professor of Religious Studies at the
University of Tromsø, Norway and the author and editor of a
number of volumes, including *The Cambridge Companion to
Religion and Terrorism.*

Margo Kitts
Hawai'i Pacific University

Margo Kitts edits the *Journal of Religion and Violence* and is
Professor and Coordinator of Religious Studies and East-West
Classical Studies at Hawai'i Pacific University in Honolulu.

ABOUT THE SERIES

Violence motivated by religious beliefs has become all too common
in the years since the 9/11 attacks. Not surprisingly, interest in the
topic of religion and violence has grown substantially since then.
This Elements series on Religion and Violence addresses this new,
frontier topic in a series of ca. fifty individual Elements. Collectively,
the volumes will examine a range of topics, including violence in
major world religious traditions, theories of religion and violence,
holy war, witch hunting, and human sacrifice, among others.

Cambridge Elements ≡

Religion and Violence

ELEMENTS IN THE SERIES

The Problem of Job and the Problem of Evil
Espen Dahl

Islam and Violence
Khaleel Mohammed

Human Sacrifice: Archaeological Perspectives from around the World
Laerke Recht

Religious Culture and Violence in Traditional China
Barend ter Haar

Mormonism and Violence: The Battles of Zion
Patrick Q. Mason

Islam and Suicide Attacks
Pieter Nanninga

Tibetan Demonology
Christopher Bell

The Bahá'í Faith, Violence, and Non-violence
Robert H. Stockman

A full series listing is available at: www.cambridge.org/ERAV

Lightning Source UK Ltd.
Milton Keynes UK
UKHW021957050820
367772UK00009B/120

9 781108 706278